HEIDEGGER'S METAHISTORY OF PHILOSOPHY

HEIDEGGER'S METAHISTORY
OF PHILOSOPHY:

Amor Fati, Being and Truth

by

BERND MAGNUS

MARTINUS NIJHOFF / THE HAGUE / 1970

ISBN 90 247 5052 0

PRINTED IN THE NETHERLANDS

For Deborah; as with all
things that really matter

TABLE OF CONTENTS

INTRODUCTION

Martin Heidegger's fame and influence are based, for the most part, on his first work, *Being and Time*. That this was to have been the first half of a larger two-volume project, the second half of which was never completed, is well known. That Heidegger's subsequent writings have been continuous developments of that project, in some sense, is generally acknowledged, although there is considerable disagreement concerning the manner in which his later works stand related to *Being and Time*. Heidegger scholars are deeply divided over that question. Some maintain that there is a sharp thematic cleavage in Heidegger's thought, so that the later works either refute or, at best, abandon the earlier themes. Others maintain that even to speak of a shift or a "reversal" in Heidegger's thinking is mistaken and argue, in consequence, that his thinking develops entirely consistently. Lastly, there are those who admit a shift in emphasis and themes in his works but introduce a principle of complementarity – the shift is said to represent a logical development of his thinking. Too often the groups resemble armed camps.

I do not wish to add more fuel to the fire by choosing sides in that dispute. No matter what the final verdict shall be, if there ever shall be one, regarding the continuity or discontinuity of Heidegger's thought, it is clear that the later works also need to be explicated and evaluated on their own merits, not only *Being and Time*. Although a few excellent studies of Heidegger's thought have appeared in English in the last decade, they tend to focus on *Being and Time* and, secondarily, on the relationship of the later works to it. To my knowledge, only one book has appeared to-date in English which treats an aspect of Heidegger's understanding of the history of philosophy, and not a single *critical* study. This book endeavors to begin to remedy that deficiency.

It is not the case that Heidegger's understanding of the history of philosophy is merely *a* theme in his works. It is *the* theme of his later works in my view. If *Being and Time* is correctly characterized as a phenomenological description of *Dasein*, of the human way of being, then Heidegger's subsequent works, in the main, attempt to show how the question of Being (*Sein*) has been (mis)understood from Plato to Nietzsche. Presumably, the tradition's failure to grasp the human way of being is grounded in its more fundamental failure to articulate clearly the sense of Being, "to be," in general. It is not at all accidental, in short, that the projected second volume of *Being and Time* was to take as its subject-matter a recapitulation and destruction of the history of ontology.[1]

This book, then, is not intended as still another introduction to the philosophy of Martin Heidegger. It is a critical analysis and exposition of the second phase of his thought.

Heidegger's provocative interpretations of the pre-Socratic philosophers, Plato, Aristotle, Descartes, Kant, Hegel, and Nietzsche, are all conditioned by his inquiry into the meaning of Being. That inquiry determines the character of his historical studies. And although there have been frequent grumblings about the "validity" of such an approach, no sustained efforts have hitherto been made to come to grips with the methodological questions which Heidegger's hermeneutic occasions.

I do not want to suggest that this study covers the full range of problems raised by Heidegger's metahistorical interpretation of the history of philosophy. It does not. I have been forced to circumscribe the range of analysis very sharply. Nietzsche is the center of gravity, point of focus, and, finally, the touchstone for Heidegger's interpretations, in this study. A number of considerations dictated this choice. First, Heidegger has devoted more attention to Nietzsche than he has to all other philosophers combined. His interpretation of Nietzsche as the last metaphysician of the West helps to account for the inordinate amount of material Heidegger has produced concerning Nietzsche. Second, as a consequence of the first, we have a more adequate basis for judging the value of Heidegger's approach to Nietzsche. Third, it is my opinion that Nietzsche's philosophy is inherently more susceptible of conflicting interpretations than is, say, Kant's or Aristotle's.

---

[1] *Sein und Zeit*. Tübingen: 7. Aufl., 1953. Cf. Introduction.

Rather than serving as a deterrent in explicating and critically assessing Heidegger's interpretation of Nietzsche, I found this to be an asset. It forces one to make difficult decisions and to be painstakingly careful in advancing an interpretation of Nietzsche, rather than merely passing on accepted, allegedly "standard" interpretations. At the same time it affords the reader a point of reference from which to compare methods of historical-textual criticism.

Nowhere are the methodological problems of interpretation more acute and more visible than in the case of Nietzsche's doctrine of eternal recurrence. We are not dealing with a theory whose meaning is clear, as it is commonly supposed. Some of the most elementary elements of the doctrine are disputed. Although Nietzsche regarded the doctrine of eternal recurrence as his most important concept, conflicting interpretations still prevail. Hence, before Heidegger's interpretation can be meaningfully assessed, an effort should be made to interpret the doctrine in the light of the texts and of previous interpretations. The first part of this study consists, therefore, of an attempted reconstruction of the eternal recurrence theory. The result of this attempted reconstruction is the conviction that excessive emphasis has hitherto been placed upon the cosmological "proof" for eternal recurrence, to the detriment of the axiological dimension which Nietzsche explored in his published works. Although such an interpretation is not necessarily irreconcilable with the more penetrating Nietzsche studies, it does suggest a fundamental change in emphasis; a change in the degree of importance we are to attach to the prescriptive as opposed to the empirical elements of the doctrine.

Heidegger's own interpretation of Nietzsche raises obvious additional difficulties. It is guided by no conventional standards of critical scholarship. For example, Heidegger views the doctrine of eternal recurrence as the last metaphysical thought in the Western tradition, the culmination and completion of metaphysics, a thought which is fated to appear when it does as Nietzsche's response to the claim of the Being (*Sein*) of beings (*Seienden*). Clearly we are dealing here with no ordinary interpretation. Heidegger's interpretation is propelled by an inner necessity of his own thinking which pursues the meaning of Being. The unorthodox character of Heidegger's approach has been succinctly expressed by William Richardson as "endeavoring to comprehend and express not what another thinker thought/said, but what he did not think/say, could not think/say, and why he could not think/say it."[2]

Heidegger's interpretation cannot be evaluated meaningfully, then, after merely having clarified Nietzsche's doctrine of eternal recurrence. A critical understanding must take the nature of Heidegger's approach into account, not merely the results of this approach.

Specifically, the first part of this study, the reconstruction of Nietzsche's doctrine of eternal recurrence, deals with three issues in succession. The problems posed by Nietzsche's literary remains, the *Nachlass*,[3] are briefly reviewed in Chapter I, followed by an extensive discussion of the cosmological proof for the doctrine of eternal recurrence, in Chapter II. Finally, the doctrine of eternal recurrence is considered metaphysically i.e., as a theory about a generic trait of entities as such. In this chapter the doctrine of eternal recurrence is interpreted as an existential imperative; a critique of metaphysics, Christianity, and nihilism.

The second part of this book, Chapter I, establishes the context within which Heidegger's interpretation operates. It deals with the interrelationship between Being, truth, and the history of Western metaphysics. Central consideration is devoted to the role that Plato plays in the transformation of truth from *alétheia* to *orthotes* and the effect of this transformation upon "metaphysic's" subsequent comprehension of Being. It is here that Heidegger's extraordinary view of metaphysics as nihilism, identified as the forgetfulness of Being, is presented. In order to properly prepare the context of Heidegger's interpretation of Nietzsche, it is pointed out that his assessment of the history of metaphysics depends to a marked degree upon a partial and inadequate reading of Plato and Descartes and, above all, upon the untenable view that truth has always meant some version of *adequatio rei et intellectus* within the history of Western philosophy.

The second chapter then turns directly to Heidegger's interpretation of the doctrine of eternal recurrence. Heidegger regards the will-to-power and the eternal recurrence as a single phenomenon, Nietzsche's conception of the Being of beings. The term "the will-to-power" expresses Being viewed as *essentia,* "eternal recurrence"

---

[2] William Richardson, *Heidegger: Through Phenomenology to Thought.* (Martinus Nijhoff: The Hague, 1963), p. 22.

[3] The term *Nachlass* will hereafter refer to volumes IX–XVI of the *Grossoktavausgabe* in either of its two complete editions; the 1895–1901 edition (Leipzig: C. G. Naumann) or the 1926 edition (Leipzig: Alfred Kröner).

denotes Being as *existentia*. The doctrine of eternal recurrence is to liberate previous reflection, the history of metaphysics, from aversion to time and transience, according to Heidegger. It is pointed out, in criticism, that the textual evidence which Heidegger presents is inadequate to sustain such a view. "Revenge," deliverance from which is viewed as a necessary condition for liberation from aversion to transience, is not exclusively a metaphysical concept, as Heidegger asserts, nor is the term "will" an ontological concept in the passages from which he quotes. The terms "revenge" and "will" function as psychological concepts in the *complete* passages from which Heidegger quotes as the basis for his interpretations.

Chapter III suggests that Heidegger's treatment of Nietzsche as the last metaphysician of the West places a burden on the theory of eternal recurrence which that doctrine cannot easily bear. It is a moot point to contend, as Heidegger does, that Nietzsche was compelled to think Being under the guise of eternal recurrence. But this *a priori* context into which Heidegger fits Nietzsche has serious consequences. First, this approach forces Heidegger to ignore altogether the cosmological proof with which Nietzsche was undoubtedly struggling. Second, it misses the depths of Nietzsche's critique of Christianity, occasioned by the concept of eternal recurrence. Third, it forces Heidegger into an untenable identification of Nietzsche's conception of nihilism with his own. Fourth, this approach misses the existential significance of the doctrine of eternal recurrence by treating it exclusively as a transvaluated Platonism.

Despite these critical remarks regarding Heidegger's metahistorical interpretation, a profound ambivalence occasionally surfaces in this study. Although it is argued that Heidegger's Nietzsche interpretation must finally be rejected, there nonetheless remains the immense suggestiveness of his approach, not to mention the light it sheds on his own philosophy. In my opinion, Heidegger's reading of the tradition, as in the case of Hegel, sheds more light on the author than on the past. But I am persuaded that Heidegger's thinking is an important achievement of twentieth century philosophy. The impulse and motive of this study is, then, not a philosophical antipathy. What motivated this study, in part, was the growing practice among Heidegger scholars – especially in France – of interpreting the great philosophers from Heidegger's point of vantage. I am persuaded that such a doctrinaire approach is ruinous to the history of philosophy as a discipline, and is foreign to Heidegger's own thinking as well.

The translations of Heidegger and Nietzsche are my own. Where these appear overly literal, I have always had some purpose in mind. More often than not, the more literal the translation the more the passage in question is in dispute. I have retained the original German throughout in footnotes, in any case, to enable the reader to compare the translations with the original. Those who lack German can compare my translations with others – where these are available.

The list of those to whom I am indebted is excessively long. Most prominently, however, I am grateful to Hannah Arendt and Jacob Taubes, for their help and encouragement when I needed it most; Albert Hofstadter, for his helpful critical reading of an earlier draft of this manuscript; Paul O. Kristeller and Richard Kuhns, for their generous reading of parts of this manuscript; The University of California, Riverside, for its supporting grants to complete this volume. Lastly, and most especially, I want to thank Arthur Danto for his constant encouragement, support, and generosity of spirit.

PART I

THE PHILOSOPHY OF ETERNAL RECURRENCE

CHAPTER I

NIETZSCHE'S LITERARY ESTATE

Nietzsche's world-view has been called "a system in aphorisms."[1] However, general agreement as to the nature of this system does not exist, due partly to the aphoristic genre itself. In fact, unanimity as to whether Nietzsche did in fact have a system does not exist either.[2] In consequence, the meaning and importance attributed to the major themes within Nietzsche's alleged system – overman, revaluation of values, the will-to-power, the eternal recurrence – have been the subject of spirited and prolonged debate.

If Nietzsche's aphoristic style, with its frequently contradictory content, has been partially responsible for the diversity of interpretations, then the controversy surrounding the first edition of his collected works has been an equal source of confusion.

The first complete edition of Nietzsche's works, the *Gesamtausgabe in Grossoktav,* was compiled over a period exceeding thirty years.[3] Prior to the onslaught of insanity in January 1889, Nietzsche had completed four works which were not published at that time. Three of the four works, *The Twilight of the Idols,*[4] *The Antichrist,*[5] and *Nietzsche contra Wagner,*[6] were incorporated into the collected

---

[1] Karl Löwith, *Nietzsches Philosophie der ewigen Wiederkehr des Gleichen* (Stuttgart: Kohlhammer, 1956), p. 15.

[2] Karl Schlechta (ed.), *Friedrich Nietzsche, Werke in drei Bänden* (München: Hanser, 1960) "Nachwort" p. 1436: "Nietzsche hat kein 'System'."

[3] The first edition of Nietzsche's collected works was begun in 1894 and completed in 1901, in fifteen volumes. The last and complete edition of the *Grossoktavausgabe* was produced in 1926. The first edition is conventionally called the Naumann edition of the *Grossoktavausgabe,* the second the Kröner edition. Since the pages of both editions virtually coincide, no distinction will be drawn in referring to these volumes. The *Grossoktavausgabe* itself will be referred to hereafter simply as the GOA.

[4] GOA VIII *Die Götzendämmerung,* pp. 59–182.

[5] GOA VIII *Der Antichrist,* pp. 213–332.

[6] GOA VIII *Nietzsche contra Wagner,* pp. 183–212.

works in 1895, which then brought the Nietzsche edition to a total of eight volumes. For a considerable period these eight volumes were thought of as constituting all the works published by Nietzsche during his lifetime, or designated by him for publication. The first edition of his "autobiographical" *Ecce Homo,* the fourth book written by Nietzsche in 1888, did not appear in print until twenty years had elapsed, 1908, and was incorporated into the GOA still later as a part of volume XV. By 1911 the GOA consisted of a total of sixteen uneven volumes; volumes I-VIII consisting of Nietzsche's published works, volumes IX-XVI containing Nietzsche's unpublished notes. Volume XV had appeared in 1901, the year after Nietzsche's death and seven years before the publication of *Ecce Homo,* containing some four hundred notes under the title *The Will-to-Power.*[7] In 1904, just three years later, a completely new edition of *The Will-to-Power* was promoted by the appearance of an additional two hundred notes from *The Will-to-Power,* in E. Forster-Nietzsche's *Das Leben Friedrich Nietzsches.*[8] Subsequent editions enlarged the controversial *The Will-to-Power* to 1067 entries.[9] By 1926 the GOA had reached twenty volumes in size, the Kröner edition, through the addition of three volumes of *Philologica* (XVII–XIX) and an index (XX).[10] This twenty volume collection has served as the first complete edition and the source of considerable dispute.

The first eight volumes of the GOA, then, contain books published by Nietzsche during his productive period, as well as books designated by him for publication which were not released until his lapse into madness. Volumes IX-XVI, on the other hand, consist of writings neither published by Nietzsche *nor* designated for publication, with the exception of *Ecce Homo.*[11] This *Nachlass* consists of heterogeneous material; material which, although written during the author's lifetime, was not incorporated into the published works, on the one hand, and material post-dating Nietzsche's last completed work, on the other hand.

Rather than serving as a basis for the clarification of Nietzsche's

---

[7] GOA *Nachlass* XV *Der Wille Zur Macht.*

[8] Elisabeth Förster-Nietzsche, *Das Leben Friedrich Nietzsches* (Leipzig: C. G. Naumann, 1904).

[9] GOA *Nachlass* XV pp. 137–489, XVI.

[10] GOA *Register Band* XX. Prepared by Richard Oehler.

[11] GOA *Nachlass* XV pp. 1–136.

position, the heterogeneity of the GOA frequently looms as a severe obstacle on the way to undistorted interpretations. If the very existence of the *Nachlass* has bequeathed problems to Nietzsche scholars which are at least resolvable in principle, the manner in which the literary remains were gathered, organized and edited, has given rise to suspicions which permanently threaten the possibility of agreement.

Without extensive details, it should be noted that the method, competence, and character of the architect of the GOA – Elisabeth Förster-Nietzsche – have been challenged, notably by Walter Kaufmann[12] and Karl Schlechta.[13] Karl Schlechta's three volume edition of Nietzsche's collected works[14] contains but one-third the number of entries from the unpublished notes than are found in the GOA. Further, no attempt is made to systematize these "notes of the 'eighties'"[15] into coherent, albeit provisional "planned" works. In his "philological Post-Script"[16] and "Epilogue,"[17] Schlechta supplies suggestive documentation in support of the thesis that Nietzsche had abandoned plans for a *magnum opus* entitled *The Will-to-Power*[18] and that much of the material appearing under that title consists of guess-work bordering not infrequently on forgery. In addition to citing petty forgeries, in the form of testimonials to Nietzsche's sister's philosophical and interpretive abilities, Schlechta discusses the considerable difficulties involved in arranging Nietzsche's notes. Since Nietzsche wrote much of the time while walking, sometimes in abbreviations of his own creation, his difficult handwriting had become practically illegible toward the end of his productive period. The task

---

[12] *Nietzsche* (Princeton: Princeton University Press, 1950), "The Nietzsche Legend."

[13] Nietzsche, *Werke in drei Bänden* (München: Hanser, 1960).

[14] *Ibid.*

[15] *Ibid.,* vol. 3, pp. 415–927.

[16] *Ibid.,* vol. 3, pp. 1383–1432.

[17] *Ibid.,* vol. 3, pp. 1433–1454.

[18] That Nietzsche had abandoned plans for *The Will-to-Power* has become a commonplace since first publicized by Walter A. Kaufmann in his *Nietzsche* (Princeton: Princeton University Press, 1950). The *Musarionausgabe* of Nietzsche's collected works contains over twenty-five plans for the disputed *The Will-to-Power* (cf. XVIII, 335–361), as well as indications that Nietzsche intended to write a major work entitled *Revaluation of all Values* instead, whose first part was to have been the already published *The Antichrist*. (cf. *Musarionausgabe* XVIII, 347 and XIX, 390–402).

of deciphering Nietzsche's jottings was assigned to Peter Gast by Elisabeth Förster-Nietzsche. Stylistic changes were frequently introduced, Schlechta claims, words or phrases changed or added, arbitrary plans followed from among many possible ones. All in all, Schlechta calls *The Will-to-Power* a *"Machwerk"* produced largely by the greed and power over Nietzsche's literary estate which Elisabeth Förster-Nietzsche possessed.

Whether Karl Schlechta's indictment is accurate or not cannot be conclusively resolved by Nietzsche scholars, even those who have ready access to the Nietzsche archives. His claims do help foster a greater sensitivity, however, to the two central problems posed by the *Nachlass*. First, despite the references to – and possible clarifications of – the major problems with which Nietzsche dealt, how faithful a record of his random notes do we find in the published GOA *Nachlass*? In short, how *accurate* is the *Nachlass*? Second, how much weight should be given to the references in the *Nachlass* in interpreting Nietzsche's philosophic position? The second question is logically and methodologically distinct from the first; even if we settled the first question, precisely because it is the literary *remains* which we are considering. The second question is of considerable importance not only when considering Nietzsche's disputed "planned" work(s), but when considering entries which Nietzsche chose *not* to incorporate into his published works, for reasons unknown to us.

It is fortunate that a substantial number of references to the doctrine of eternal recurrence exist in Nietzsche's published works. If one were to start from the published works, the importance attached to passages in the literary remains is diminished. Nonetheless, the number of distinct references to the doctrine of eternal recurrence found in the *Nachlass* is more than four times greater[19] than references found in the published works.[20] And it is of some importance to observe in this connection that *nowhere* in the works published by Nietzsche or designated for publication by him is there an attempt made to present the doctrine of eternal recurrence explicitly in terms of an empirical-cosmological hypothesis.

---

[19] There are more than forty-four distinct sections dealing with the eternal recurrence in the GOA *Nachlass*.

[20] GOA I–VIII. Approximately ten uneven sections deal principally with the doctrine of eternal recurrence. Their length varies enormously.

This point has a significant bearing upon the thesis presented in the following chapters. The position I shall develop maintains, in simplest terms, that the doctrine of eternal recurrence was conceived by Nietzsche primarily as an existential doctrine, which I shall call an existential imperative, for which he subsequently (and unsuccessfully) sought empirical justification. The relevant issues affecting this interpretation can be exhibited somewhat more clearly if the interpretive problem is stated within the general context of the fact-value split.

Almost all Nietzsche scholars agree that the doctrine of eternal recurrence advances the view that, in fact, everything eternally recurs, *and* that we ought to behave as if it does. Clearly, the first part is a descriptive hypothesis, the second is prescriptive. In presenting Nietzsche's position, however, previous scholars have generally emphasized the descriptive hypotheses and have tended to assimilate the prescriptive to it. Although both empirical and normative elements are present, the position for which I argue below is that the prevailing emphasis ought to be reversed. The empirical hypothesis should be assimilated to, and understood as occasioned by, the prescriptive dimension of the doctrine of eternal recurrence. The principal textual reason for suggesting this change in emphasis is that Nietzsche elected to publish the non-cosmological arguments while, *at the same time,* withholding the empirical formulations. A complementary reason for suggesting this procedure is that the unpublished empirical arguments are no less ambiguous and subject to interpretation, in my judgment, than are the non-cosmological formulations. The methodology advanced, then, takes the published position as the principal source of evidence and the *Nachlass* as an aid to clarifying that position. Although no *radically* new interpretation will emerge as a consequence of this method, the reversal will bring other doctrinal elements into sharper relief. Specifically, the doctrine of eternal recurrence will be seen as a critique and alternative to metaphysics, Christianity, and nihilism, as Nietzsche conceived them. Moreover, this will be viewed as the central task of the doctrine, rather than an interesting side effect.

It may be necessary to repeat that the methodology adopted and the interpretation which it suggests do not necessarily nullify prevailing interpretations. But they do change the points of emphasis in a fundamental way. Equally clearly, this interpretation is not designed to eliminate any real or alleged inconsistencies in Nietzsche's doctrine of eternal recurrence. It does suggest, however, that Nietzsche was alive to most of the *prima facie* inconsistencies which his critics claim to have found and that, in spite of this, he regarded the doctrine as his most significant concept. Moreover, in this case, as in many others, I think Nietzsche's judgment was superior to that of his critics.

CHAPTER II

COSMOLOGICAL AND LOGICAL DIMENSIONS OF THE DOCTRINE OF ETERNAL RECURRENCE

In *Ecce Homo,* in which Nietzsche ambiguously reviewed his philosophical development, the origin of the doctrine of eternal recurrence is cited: "The concept of eternal recurrence belongs in August of the year 1881. It was written on a page with the inscription: '6000 feet beyond man and time.' I went through the forests at the lake of Silvaplana on that day . . . there the thought came to me."[1]

Not only is there disagreement as to the meaning of this idea; some Nietzsche scholars have rejected the entire concept either as a religious experience[2] opaque to philosophical analysis, or worse still as "a deceptively mocking mystery of delusion."[3] The overwhelming evidence indicates, on the contrary, that Nietzsche regarded the doctrine of eternal recurrence as his most significant concept.[4] Nietzsche regarded the doctrine as "the most scientific of all possible hypotheses,"[5] and Zarathustra as its prophet: "I now relate the story of Zarathustra. The basic conception of this work (is) *the eternal recurrence notion.*"[6]

For purposes of analysis, we can consider the doctrine of eternal

[1] GOA XV *Ecce Homo,* 85: "Der Ewige Wiederkunftsgedanke gehört in den August des Jahres 1881; er ist auf ein Blatt hingeworfen mit der Unterschrift: '6000 Fuss jenseits von Mensch und Zeit.' Ich ging an jenem Tage am See von Silvaplana durch die Wälder . . . da kam mir dieser Gedanke."

[2] Alfred Baeumler, *Nietzsche der Philosoph und Politiker* (Leipzig: Reclam, 1931).

[3] Ernst Bertram, *Nietzsche: Versuch einer Mythologie* (Berlin: Georg Bondi, 1918), p. 12.

[4] Cf. GOA VI 321; GOA *Nachlass* XII 371; XIII 264, 415, XV 86, 182; XVI 398.

[5] GOA *Nachlass* XV 182: "Die Wissenschaftlichste aller möglichen Hypothesen."

[6] GOA XV *Ecce Homo,* 85: "Ich erzähle nunmehr die Geschichte des Zarathustra. Die Grundconception des Werkes, der Ewige-Wiederkunfts-Gedanke . . ."

recurrence from two points of vantage: the empirical, and the axiological. In the final analysis, this distinction is neither generic nor is it intended to be very rigorous. The descriptive version, for example, is frequently referred to below as either "empirical," "cosmological" or "descriptive." The "axiological" is sometimes called the "ethical" or "postulational." On the other hand, the terms are not mutually exclusive either. If, for example, the cosmos consists of a finite number of energy configurations which recur eternally, and if human actions are conceived by Nietzsche as a part of any given configuration, then human actions too are "fated" within the eternal recurrence. Here the cosmology of the doctrine implies a corresponding axiology, and the distinction between the two ultimately collapses. Conversely, if human action is our starting point, and it is conceived under the yoke of eternal recurrence, this implies a rather strict deterministic scheme of nature. In this case, the axiology would imply a corresponding cosmology and the distinction would, once again, ultimately collapse. This two-fold distinction, therefore, is valuable primarily in differentiating the *emphasis* of each Nietzsche entry which deals with the doctrine of eternal recurrence. Thus, for example, when Nietzsche asserts that "the task is to live in such a way that you must wish to live again"[7] we would regard this as an axiological entry. Where, on the other hand, Nietzsche argues entirely from empirical considerations, i.e., finite energy, space, matter, infinite time, we would regard such entries as primarily cosmological/empirical. The interpretive question, for us, is to try to ascertain, if possible, which emphasis receives the greatest stress and why – the empirical, or the axiological.

As was said before, of the two dimensions to which this doctrine belongs no sustained argument for the cosmological status of eternal recurrence exists in any work published by Nietzsche or authorized for publication by him. References to the empirical requirements of the doctrine of eternal recurrence are found only in the *Nachlass*.

Specifically, the two sources in which the doctrine of eternal recurrence is unmistakably presented as an empirical hypothesis is in the notes[8] from the period in which Nietzsche wrote *The Gay Science,* and in the disputed *The Will-to-Power*.[9] This fact is noteworthy in

---

[7] GOA *Nachlass* XII, 64: ... so leben, dass du wünschen musst, wieder zu leben, ist die Aufgabe.

[8] GOA *Nachlass* XII, 1–235.

[9] GOA *Nachlass* XV, XVI.

itself; first, because Nietzsche presented the doctrine of eternal recurrence in the published version of *The Gay Science* in axiological and not cosmological terms; second, because of the shroud of uncertainty surrounding the accuracy of the references found in *The Will-to-Power*. Yet, the majority of Nietzsche studies treat the cosmological version of the doctrine with at least the same degree of emphasis as the axiological intention.

The issue here is not one of rendering a judgment as to whether Nietzsche intended the cosmological/empirical version of the doctrine of eternal recurrence to play a vital role in the clarification of this difficult notion. We shall merely stress a distinction in what follows between Nietzsche's published reflections concerning the doctrine of eternal recurrence and that version, the empirical, which he chose to withhold from publication.

The three entries in which the eternal recurrence is presented as a cosmological hypothesis have been variously interpreted. Since much of the cosmological argument depends on these three formulations, they are presented here:

The amount of total energy is determined, not infinite. Let us beware of such conceptual aberrations! Consequently, the number of states, changes, combinations and developments of this energy is incredibly large and practically unmeasurable, but nonetheless determined and not infinite. However, time, in which the totality exerts its energy, is infinite. That is, energy is eternally equal and eternally active. Up to this moment an infinity has passed, i.e., all possible developments must already have come to pass. Consequently, the present development must be a repetition and also the one which bore it and the one which will originate from it, and so on forward and backward! Everything has come to pass in so far as the total configuration of all energy eternally recurs. Whether, quite aside from that, anything identical has come to pass is entirely indemonstrable. It would appear that the configuration structures attributes anew in the greatest detail, so that two different configurations cannot contain anything identical. Whether anything identical can exist within a configuration, for example two leaves – I doubt it . . .[10]

---

[10] GOA *Nachlass* XII, 51–52: "Das Mass der All-Kraft ist bestimmt, nichts 'Unendliches': hüten wir uns vor solchen Ausschweifungen des Begriffs! Folglich ist die Zahl der Lagen, Veränderungen, Combinationen und Entwicklungen dieser Kraft zwar ungeheuer gross und practisch 'unermesslich,' aber jedenfalls bestimmt und nicht unendlich. Wohl aber ist die Zeit, in der das All seine Kraft übt, unendlich, das heisst, die Kraft ist ewig gleich und ewig thätig: – bis diesen Augenblick ist schon eine Unendlichkeit abgelaufen, das heisst alle möglichen Entwicklungen müssen schon dagewesen sein. Folglich muss die augenblickliche

The external world of energies leads back to a simplest state of these energies; and also forward to a simplest state. Could not and must not both states be identical? Out of a system of fixed energies, i.e., out of a measurable energy, no innumerability of states can arise. Only in the case of the false presupposition of an infinite space, in which energies evaporate as it were, is the last state an unproductive one, a dead one.[11]

If an equilibrium of energy had ever been reached it would still exist. Thus, it never occurred. The present state contradicts such an assumption. (However,) if one assumes that a state has existed absolutely the same as the present one, this assumption would not be contradicted by the present state. But, among the infinite possibilities this must have been the case because an eternity has already passed until now . . . And, if the present state has already occurred, then also the one which bore it and the one which preceded it and so on, backward. From this there emerges the fact that it has already occurred a second and third time; also, that it will occur a second and third time – innumerable times, backward and forward. That is, all becoming moves in a fixed number of entirely identical states . . . Assuming an incredible number of cases, arriving accidentally at the identical condition is more probable than (arriving at) the absolutely never identical.[12]

Entwicklung eine Wiederholung sein und so die, welche sie gebar und die, welche aus ihr entsteht und so vorwärts und rückwärts weiter! Alles ist unzählige Male dagewesen, insofern die Gesamtlage aller Kräfte immer wiederkehrt. Ob je, davon abgesehen, irgend etwas Gleiches dagewesen ist, ist ganz unerweislich. Es scheint, dass die Gesamtlage bis in's Kleinste hinein die Eigenschaften neu bildet, so dass zwei verschiedene Gesamtlagen nichts Gleiches haben können. Ob es in einer Gesamtlage etwas Gleiches geben kann, zum Beispiel zwei Blätter? Ich zweifle . . ."

[11] *Ibid.,* 55: "Die vorhandene Welt von Kräften leitet zurück auf einen einfachsten Zustand dieser Kräfte: und ebenso vorwärts auf einen einfachsten Zustand, – könnten und müssten beide Zustände nicht identisch sein? Aus einem System bestimmter Kräfte, also aus einer messbar sicheren Kraft kann sich keine Unzähligkeit der Zustände ergeben. Nur bei der falschen Annahme eines unendlichen Raumes, in welchen sich die Kraft gleichsam verflüchtigt, ist der letzte Zustand ein unproductiver, todter."

[12] *Ibid.,* 55–56: "Wäre ein Gleichgewicht der Kraft irgendwann einmal erreicht worden, so dauerte es noch: also ist es nie eingetreten. Der augenblickliche Zustand widerspricht der Annahme. Nimmt man an, es habe einmal einen Zustand gegeben, absolut gleich dem augenblicklichen, so wird diese Annahme nicht durch den augenblicklichen Zustand widersprochen. In den unendlichen Möglichkeiten muss es aber diesen Fall gegeben haben, denn bis jetzt ist schon eine Unendlichkeit verflossen. Wenn das Gleichgewicht möglich wäre, so müsste es eingetreten sein. – Und wenn dieser augenblickliche Zustand da war, dann auch der, der ihn gebar, und dessen Vorzustand u.s.w. zurück, – daraus ergiebt sich, dass er auch ein zweites und drittes Mal schon da war – ebenso dass er ein zweites, drittes Mal da sein wird, – unzählige Male, vorwärts und rückwärts. Das heisst es bewegt sich alles Werden in der Wiederholung einer bestimmten Zahl vollkommen gleicher Zustände . . . denn, eine ungeheure Masse von Fällen

Let us extract at least the following broad assumptions for the doctrine of eternal recurrence as a cosmological hypothesis from the above three entries: Nietzsche assumes that space is finite, that energy is finite, and that time is infinite.[13] From these three assumptions there follows a fourth for Nietzsche, namely, that no terminal state in the configuration of energy has ever been reached.[14] Since space and energy are finite, it follows for Nietzsche that only a finite number of configurations unfold in an eternity of time, and that any given configurations must, in consequence, occur eternally: "the eternal recurrence of the same." Moreover, the same configuration not only will recur eternally but actually has occurred an infinite number of previous times. This moment, thus, is but one repetition of an infinite number of identical moments in the "past" and is fated to recur eternally in the "future."

Arthur Danto has made a close study of the logical status of Nietzsche's assumptions in a recent book, and has reduced the premises in the quoted first entry to three:[15] "1. The sum total of energy in the universe is finite. 2. The number of states of energy is finite. 3. Energy is conserved."[16] Since these three propositions are logically independent, Danto adds four more which are needed to generate the sort of argument Nietzsche has in mind. "4. Time is infinite. 5. Energy has infinite duration. . Change is eternal. 7. Principle of Sufficient Reason."[17] Whether any or all of these additional premises are explicitly contained in the entries is not at issue here, although it would appear that premise number four is explicitly present in the material from which Arthur Danto quotes: "However, time, in which the totality exerts its energy, is infinite."[18] Premise number five may also be present in embryonic form in the phrase: "energy is eternally equal and eternally active." Whether any or all of these premises are explicitly present in Nietzsche's formulations is of minor importance.

---

vorausgesetzt, ist die zufällige Erreichung des gleichen Wurfes wahrscheinlicher als die absolute Nie-Gleichheit."

[13] GOA *Nachlass* XII, 51. Questions concerning the plausibility of these assumptions within the context of 19th or 20th century physics does not concern us here and will, consequently, be omitted from discussion.

[14] *Ibid.*, 55–56.

[15] Arthur Danto, *Nietzsche as Philosopher.* (New York: Macmillan Co., 1965).

[16] *Ibid.*, p. 206.

[17] *Ibid.*, pp. 207–208.

[18] *Ibid.*, p. 205.

Of principal importance, for us, is the question whether Nietzsche intended to present an unequivocal argument for *identical* recurrences in the above quoted entries. By "intended" we do not mean "Did Nietzsche *want to* present an argument for identical recurrences?" We mean, rather, was it Nietzsche's purpose to formulate a consistent empirical doctrine of eternal recurrence in these entries? The so-called "classic" first entry may not be the summation of a considered position, although virtually all Nietzsche scholars have taken it to be *the* presentation and basis of the cosmological version of eternal recurrence. The uncritical manner in which that formulation has been judged to be an empirical/cosmological argument is unfortunate.

The conclusion of the first entry, XII 51–52, has received inadequate attention. "Whether, quite aside from that, anything identical has come to pass is entirely indemonstrable. It would appear that the configuration structures attributes anew in the greatest detail, so that two different configurations cannot contain anything identical. Whether anything identical can exist within a configuration, for example two leaves – I doubt it." [19]

These three concluding sentences, which have been universally ignored, need at least as much attention as do the preceding ones, in my opinion, since their meaning is unclear. The conclusion of entry XII 51 could be interpreted in at least two incompatible ways, either as consistent or inconsistent with the remainder of the entry. [20] I shall argue that these last three sentences of that entry, when subjected to careful textual analysis, express a halting doubt about the adequacy of the cosmological/empirical formulation of the doctrine of eternal recurrence, rather than a consistent formulation.

Having argued that energy is finite, that the states (*Lagen*), changes, and evolutions of energy are likewise finite, and that these states unfold in an eternity of time, Nietzsche says: "Everything has come to pass in so far as the total configuration of all energy eternally recurs." [21] The next three sentences, if *consistent* with the preceding ones, would then assert the following: (1) The sentence, "Whether,

---

[19] GOA XII, 51–52.

[20] I am grateful to Arthur Danto for pointing out to me that the last three lines need not be read as inconsistent with the preceding material and for suggesting a line of argument which would eliminate the apparent contradiction. It should be added also that this argument as presented is my own and that different formulations of it might perhaps be more persuasive.

[21] GOA *Nachlass* XII, 51–52.

quite aside from that, anything identical has come to pass is entirely indemonstrable,"[22] would mean, simply, that it is impossible to give empirical evidence in support of the eternal recurrence hypothesis. The phrase "davon abgesehen" would mean "quite aside from the fact that the total configuration of all energy eternally recurs." In short, the sentence could easily be rendered, "Whether anything identical has come to pass is entirely indemonstrable, apart from the fact that the total configuration of all energy eternally recurs." This interpretation would be consistent with the remainder of the entry, since the doctrine would then *a priori* preclude the possibility of finding empirical evidence as support. Since identical recurrent world-states would exist within all configurations, every item of evidence in one state would have an identical counterpart in every other world-state. Stated differently, in the absence of differential empirical evidence, we cannot demonstrate the existence of an earlier identical world-state, because the evidence required is identical within each world-state. An identity of indiscernibles thus holds within any configuration. The thrust of this interpretation would therefore be directed exclusively at the impossibility of giving a proof, *any* empirical proof I should add, of the hypothesis. (2) The next sentence ("It would appear that the configuration structures attributes anew in the greatest detail, so that two different configurations cannot contain anything identical") would mean, then, that two discreet world-states (A and B) do not possess an identical content since they are *different* – since "the configuration structures attributes anew in the greatest detail." (3) The final sentence, then, merely asserts that the same rule applies within a given configuration (A or B) – that no identical elements are to be found within a *single* configuration.

An interpretation of this sort renders the entire quoted entry consistent. It argues that Nietzsche is advancing three things: first, the indemonstrability of the eternal recurrence hypothesis by empirical means (the indemonstrability of the alleged fact that the existence of configuration A supports the existence of an earlier configuration A); second, the existence of more than one discreet configuration (at least A and B) in which all elements are differentiated and between which there is no carry-over; and, third, that within any configuration (A or B) its content is sufficiently diversified so as to preclude identities within elements of that configuration ("for example, two leaves").

[22] *Ibid.*

Such an interpretation, however *prima facie* plausible, must first be related to the text and the terms it introduces. Specifically, what does the term *Gesamtlage* (configuration) mean, and what is its relationship to the term *Lage* (state)? Does the term "two different configurations" refer to configurations in the sense of disjuncts A or B?

The term *Gesamtlage* is first introduced in the sentence which precedes the three concluding sentences.[23] It appears only in these sentences. It refers, specifically, to "the total configuration of all energy." Before introducing the term, Nietzsche had spoken of the relationship between two orders of phenomena. On the one hand we have "Das Mass der All-Kraft" (the total amount of energy), and on the other hand we have the various states (*Lagen*), changes (*Veränderungen*), developments (*Entwicklungen*) and combinations (*Combinationen*) of this energy. If the term *Gesamtlage* refers to either order of phenomena, which it clearly does, it refers to the former and not the latter. That is, it refers to the *gesamte Lagen*, hence *Gesamtlage*, of energy – the total ensemble of states. It would, therefore, be simply incorrect to assume that the term "configuration" (*Gesamtlage*) can be employed in the same sense as the term *Lage* (state) and its equivalents. The term introduces not a given configuration among many (A or B, etc.) but the total *ensemble* of these states. It is a macrocosmic and not a microcosmic term.

To clarify this point, let us conceive of three states (*Lagen*) of energy – each one corresponding to an historical period, A, B, and C. To render each one more graphically, let A represent the period from the dawn of human life to the beginnings of recorded, written, history; let B represent the period from recorded history to the death of Socrates; let C represent the period from 399 B.C. to Nietzsche's discovery of the eternal recurrence in 1881.

Each phase, A, B, C, represents a *Lage* (state), according to Nietzsche.[24] Nietzsche subsequently and consistently uses the term *Zustand*

---

[23] *Ibid.*

[24] The identification of A, B, C, with "states," rather than "configurations" becomes obvious when one reflects upon the fact that "states" constitute transformations of the "Mass der All-Kraft" and are therefore theoretically distinguishable. Whether the "total ensemble of states" (*Gesamtlage*) is equally differentiable is doubtful, since the term seems to be introduced as an equivalent for "das Mass der All-Kraft." If we interpret this correctly, the term "das Mass der All-Kraft" refers to energy quantitatively, while *Gesamtlage* refers to this energy when structured into specifiable states.

for a specific energy state (*Lage*) in the material quoted above.[25] Each state (*Lage* or *Zustand*) is a change, development, or combination of the amount of total energy. "Consequently," says Nietzsche, "the present development [(C)] is but a repetition and also the one which bore it [(B)] . . ."[26] It is at this point that the term *Gesamtlage* is introduced: "Everything has come to pass in so far as the total configuration of all energy (*Gesamtlage aller Kräfte*) eternally recurs."[27] Does the term here still mean A *or* B *or* C? Certainly not. The term, here, should mean A, B, and C, taken collectively. Each individual *Lage* (A, or B, or C) forms a link in the *Gesamtlage aller Kräfte*. The words *Lage, Entwicklung, Veränderung, Combination* and *Zustand*, are fairly well interchangeable without loss of sense precisely because – as modalities of energy – they are the forms energy can assume. And the forms which this one energy assumes, the ensemble of its states, is the *Gesamtlage aller Kräfte* – the total configuration of all energy. Note also that the term *Gesamtlage* is singular – as indeed it ought to be. The sum of the *Lagen* forms one *Gesamtlage*. Parenthetically, the plural, *Gesamtlagen*, is not introduced until the next-to-last sentence of this entry and raises an additional difficulty in understanding Nietzsche's formulation. Up to the next-to-last sentence, then, Nietzsche seems to be talking about two orders of phenomena, the "whole" and its "parts." The "parts" are the *Lagen* (states) and their transformation, the "whole" is the *Mass der All-Kraft* or the *Gesamtlage aller Kräfte*. Thus, *Lagen* A, B, C constitute the *Gesamtlage* A-B-C.

If the above interpretation is accurate, the first of the three concluding sentences asserts something like this. (1) Whether anything identical has ever come to pass – apart from the hypothetical recurrence of *Gesamtlage* A-B-C – is indemonstrable. (2) The next sentence introduces the plural form, *Gesamtlagen*, and declares that "It would appear that the *Gesamtlage* structures attributes anew in the greatest detail, so that two different *Gesamtlagen* [(pl.)] cannot contain anything identical."[28] This sentence is puzzling. On the one hand, says Nietzsche, it would appear that a *Gesamtlage* (A-B-C) structures its attributes (A and its content, B and its content, C and its content)

[25] Cf. GOA XII, 54–56, above.
[26] GOA *Nachlass* XII, 51–52.
[27] *Ibid.*
[28] *Ibid.*

in such a way that two distinct *Gesamtlagen* share nothing identical. This is odd. On the basis of the hypothesis Nietzsche had just presented, one would have to conclude that *any* two *Gesamtlagen* would have to "contain something identical." In terms of our illustration, *Gesamtlage* A-B C could recur in any sequence within the following order: A-B-C, A-C-B, B-A-C, B-C-A, C-A-B, C-B-A. This would seem to follow from Nietzsche's argument. But in that case any "two different *Gesamtlagen*" would have to share, at a minimum, a specific *Lage* – A or B or C. To rescue the apparent inconsistency we would, it seems to me, either have to eliminate the distinction between *Lage* and *Gesamtlage,* or we would have to show that the distinction does not, in fact, materially affect the argument. Since the first alternative seriously alters the text, perhaps the second alternative is a viable one.

We might want to suggest that the distinction between *Lage* and *Gesamtlage* is a different sort of relationship of "part" to "whole." In terms of our illustration, we might want to identify a *Lage* as an event within a *Gesamtlage*; for instance, the death of Socrates (*Lage*) as an event in *Gesamtlage* B. In that case, the doctrine of eternal recurrence would assert that discreet world-events (*Lagen*) recur because the *Gesamtlage* eternally recurs. The difficulty here is that it would become completely impossible to speak of the plural *Gesamtlagen* in this case. If a *Lage* is a discreet world-event, and a *Gesamtlage* is the ensemble of *Lagen,* how can there be more than one ensemble of *all* discreet world-events? In this interpretation, either *Gesamtlage* A or B or C is the *only* possible ensemble of *Lagen,* or we wind up with the dilemma suggested by the earlier interpretation. If we admit three (or more) *Gesamtlagen* containing discreet world-events, the recurring *Gesamtlagen* would have to duplicate one another.

If we now reflect on the next-to-last sentence of the entry, we are left with at least two alternatives. Either Nietzsche has introduced an inconsistency in the formulation of which he is unaware, or he is aware of some difficulty. I prefer to suggest that Nietzsche was probably aware of *some* inadequacy in the argument (even if it is not the one advanced here) and, in consequence, chose not to publish it in any shape or form. If this is a plausible view, any number of ambiguities in his cosmological formulation may have given rise to Nietzsche's reluctance to develop it further and, ultimately, to publish his discovery. For example, in addition to the apparent inconsistency which a distinction between *Lagen* and *Gesamtlage* introduces, there is an ambiguity suggested by the sentence "Everything has come to pass in so far as the *Gesamtlage aller Kräfte* eternally recurs."[29] In the opening passages of the entry under discussion, Nietzsche had asserted that a finite number of *Lagen* constitute eternally recurring moments of one sum of energy (*All-Kraft*). Nietzsche merely asserts that there are a finite number of such *Lagen*. No attempt to justify this assertion is made, beyond the declaration that a finite amount of energy, somehow, implies a finite number of energy states. In the sentence quoted above, however, the finite number of *Lagen* is made to depend most explicitly upon the eternal recurrence of the *Gesamtlage* (everything recurs because – "in so far as" – the *Gesamtlage* recurs). This introduces an important source of errors. For, the mere finiteness of energy does not entail a finite number of possible configurations of this energy, as Arthur Danto has shown.[30] If Nietzsche's formulation of the doctrine of eternal recurrence is based on the fact that energy is finite, then he is simply mistaken in deducing a finite number of world-states from it. As Arthur Danto points out, "The series $1 + \frac{1}{2} + \frac{1}{4} + \frac{1}{8} \ldots$ sums to a finite number 2. But there is not a finite number of members in the series."[31] But, and this is an interesting feature of Nietzsche's argument, the notion of a finite quantity of energy is silently dropped subsequently in favor of a *Gesamtlage* of this energy. In consequence, the sentence "Everything has come to pass in so far as the *Gesamtlage* of all energy eternally recurs," introduces a new material condition. In this formulation, the number of *Lagen* (states) is finite *not* because the amount of energy is finite, but because the ensemble, collection, of *Lagen* is a finite number. Of course, the argument is circular. It merely asserts a finite number of members in the class *Gesamtlage,* because the set consists of a finite number of members.

If we now step back from the argument, as it were, it seems that we have opened a pandora's box. If Nietzsche had perhaps scribbled the term *Gesamtlage* in haste, he would have fallen into an invalid deduction by eliminating it and speaking only of the relationship of "states" to the totality of energy. On the other hand, by introducing the term, he begs the question by assuming that a finite energy sum consists of a finite number of energy *states*.

[29] *Ibid.*
[30] Arthur Danto, *Nietzsche as Philosopher* (Macmillan, 1965), p. 206.
[31] *Ibid.*

As suggested above, Nietzsche may have been aware of the difficulties in the argument. Perhaps, and this is unsupported speculation, the term *Gesamtlage* was introduced specifically to avoid the assumption that a finite sum of energy entails a finite number of energy states.

The next-to-last sentence of entry XII 51–52, if inconsistent, or ambiguous, or both, could now perhaps be read in a new light. In light of the above considerations it is important to remember that this sentence follows two crucial sentences which could now be read to mean:

    (1) "Everything has come to pass in so far as the total configuration (*Gesamtlage*) of all energy eternally recurs." (That is, the sole reason for affirming the eternal recurrence hypothesis is that the *Gesamtlage* eternally recurs. There is no evidence to justify the claim that the finite sum of energy necessarily consists of a finite ensemble of energy states, and yet this must be assumed if we are to argue for eternal recurrence.)

    (2) "Whether, quite aside from that, anything identical has come to pass is entirely indemonstrable." (That is, *there is no way* to demonstrate the recurrence of anything if we do not first *assume* that the finite sum of energy is a sum whose members are also finite. Only on the assumption of a *Gesamtlage aller Kräfte,* a finite total ensemble of states of energy, can we even entertain the hypothesis.)

Within this context, the next-to-last sentence may be read as expressing Nietzsche's own reservations about the cogency of his formulation. In short, it could be read as an attempt to relate the hypothesis to the testimony of experience. In this light, the sentence asserts that any *Gesamtlage* is so rich in novelty and detail that two *Gesamtlagen* cannot possibly contain anything identical. In short, there are no good empirical reasons for suggesting the hypothesis in the first place. If experience were to suggest some reason for adopting the theory, *as a cosmology,* then Nietzsche would at least have found it plausible. As it stands, however, it seems that each *Gesamtlage,* configuration, structures its *Lagen,* states, in such a way that we have only novelty rather than identities. If such a reading of the next-to-last sentence is plausible, the last line merely elaborates on this point. That is, the last sentence asserts that it seems doubtful that anything identical exists in a *Gesamtlage*; even leaves are not identical!

To sum up: if Nietzsche's distinction between *Lage* and *Gesamtlage* is accidental and irrelevant, his formulation becomes a *reductio ad absurdum* which asserts, in effect, that a finite number of energy states recur eternally because . . . a finite number of energy states recur. Or, again if we ignore the distinction, Nietzsche is simply wrong. A finite sum of energy does not entail a finite number of energy states. Since the distinction introduced by the term *Gesamtlage* appears in the last four sentences and thereafter the term silently slips from view, we are perhaps justified in attaching importance to it. In any case, it cannot be ignored. If, then, the distinction between *Lagen, Gesamtlage,* and *Gesamtlagen* is significant, the argument is, at a minimum, a *petitio principii* and, at worst, inconsistent.

In the light of these considerations, coupled with the fact that these are unpublished entries, I have suggested that Nietzsche may have been aware of the difficulties in the formulation, and an attempt was made to interpret the last three lines as the expression of such an awareness. But perhaps Nietzsche expressed his own reservation about the persuasiveness of his formulation more poignantly than we have done, in a note which follows the quoted material, XII 58: "Isn't the existence of any variation at all in the world which surrounds us, rather than complete circularity, already a sufficient refutation of a uniform circularity of all that exists?" [32]

I have spent a perhaps excessive amount of time considering the last three sentences of entry XII 51–52, primarily to show that the cosmological/empirical argument was written more in the spirit of a thought-experiment – and many of Nietzsche's notes assume this character – than as a sustained argument in support of a definite position. The reason for doing this, as has been stated earlier, is to point out that previous interpretations have relied too heavily on the cosmological hypothesis, assuming that it possessed a greater degree of intelligibility and freedom from ambiguity than do the prescriptive formulations of the doctrine of eternal recurrence. I do not mean to imply, of course, that the cosmological argument is of no value in understanding Nietzsche's admittedly difficult teaching. But the methodology espoused here subordinates its importance to those reflections concerning the doctrine of eternal recurrence which Nietzsche

---

[32] GOA *Nachlass* XII, 58: "Ist nicht die Existenz irgend welcher Verschiedenheit und nicht völliger Kreisförmigkeit in der uns umgebenden Welt schon ein ausreichender Gegenbeweis gegen eine gleichmässige Kreisform alles Bestehenden?"

chose to publish. This seemingly obvious methodological precept has been virtually universally violated by Nietzsche scholars.

What would an eternally recurring configuration mean in the light of the above quoted cosmological entries? Would it mean that *identical* experience patterns recur eternally? If the number of *possible* configurations is finite, does this imply that logically *possible* as well as empirically actual configurations repeat themselves eternally? If the river flows eternally to the sea, does the sea flow to the river an equal eternity, since it is a "possible" configuration? Did Nietzsche imply a continuity between man and nature in this formulation? If so, would behavior at a given moment in time recur eternally? Am I condemned to write this sentence forever, even upon completion? Are the unrealized alternatives we have rejected in our lives and in history chosen eternally, since they constitute logically *possible* configurations, which are presumably finite in number?

These questions are not rhetorical. They are raised because they are left unanswered in the formulations found in the *Nachlass*. And yet, Nietzsche scholars who rightly take the doctrine of eternal recurrence seriously, are unanimous in ignoring a central methodological distinction between "published" and "unpublished" Nietzsche when considering the doctrine of eternal recurrence. For example, Karl Löwith, among the most thorough and penetrating Nietzsche scholars, expresses his faith in the empirical/cosmological version of the doctrine of eternal recurrence by claiming: "This effort toward a scientific foundation is no extraordinary detour, but the necessary consequence of the fact that Nietzsche wanted to teach something. A communicable philosophic doctrine cannot be content with the mere reference to an ecstatic vision or a rough sketch. The attempt at a natural-scientific foundation for the eternal recurrence, as the temporal structure of the physical world, is to be taken no less seriously than the other attempt to develop it as an ethical postulate." [33] Yet, it is not clear to me that "Nietzsche wanted to teach something," in Löwith's sense, nor is it clear that he intended to teach the eternal recurrence "as the temporal structure of the physical world," which would presumably exempt man from this formulation.

It should be clear from the above, that questions concerning an

---

[33] *Nietzsches Philosophie der ewigen Wiederkehr des Gleichen* (Stuttgart: Kohlhammer, 1956), p. 98.

unambiguous empirical formulation find no easy answers. For example, it is not clear whether an energy configuration implies simply a structural whole (*All-Kraft*) whose content is infinitely variable. If this were the case, the question of how then to relate this notion to the ethical dimension in which identical *contents* eternally recur, would pose an insuperable obstacle. If the cosmological formulation is interpreted to mean that nature, understood in its narrow sense (not *physis*), eternally recurs within inviolable cycles – day and night, Summer, Fall, Winter, and Spring – then the doctrine is reduced to a commonplace from which is well nigh impossible to derive significant axiological theses. Why, then, would Nietzsche have valued it so highly?

The most significant problem which underlies Nietzsche's theory is how we are to understand the relationship between the empirical and axiological dimensions of the doctrine of eternal recurrence. The view that Nietzsche's cosmological argument, as dissected earlier, was not intended as the "physical" basis for the doctrine does not dispose of the problem. For, when Nietzsche states the doctrine in the imperative mood – that we ought to act as if this moment eternally recurs – he almost invariably adds a declarative – that it will recur anyway. Those entries in which the primary emphasis is axiological nonetheless assert a cyclical cosmology. If we begin, therefore, with the cosmology of eternal recurrence we are required to ask what axiological consequences, if any, it entails. Most Nietzsche scholars who were earnestly troubled by the dichotomy in the doctrine have merely assumed that human action is governed by eternal recurrence, as a consequence of the cosmology. If we assume that the axiology is a deductive consequence of the cosmology, however, severe difficulties arise. The dangers inherent in assuming an *a priori* connection between the cosmology and axiology have been succinctly expressed by Arthur Danto; "The relationship between science and philosophy is complex, and the validity of inferences which run from one to the other is utterly vulnerable to attack." [34] These cautionary words suggest that if Nietzsche had "deduced" an axiology of eternal recurrence from a cosmology of eternal recurrence – based upon something more than an alleged psychological reaction – he would have required a host of additional premises.

[34] Arthur Danto, *Nietzsche as Philosopher* (New York: Macmillan, 1965), p. 208.

One could, of course, argue as Danto does, that Nietzsche's references to the doctrine of eternal recurrence such as, "My doctrine declares: the task is to live in such a way that you must wish to live again – you will anyway!,"[35] express his peculiar psychological reaction to his own cosmology. I, for one, find such an argument utterly unconvincing, and for several reasons. First, because such a causal argument presupposes that the discovery of the doctrine of eternal recurrence as an empirical cosmology is temporally prior to (cause of) other formulations. The *Nachlass* does not support such a claim.[36] At best, it supports the view that in 1881 Nietzsche formulated the doctrine of eternal recurrence as an axiology and cosmology. Which came first is a moot point. Second, we would have to assume that Nietzsche was satisfied with the adequacy of the empirical formulation he had jotted down in his notes. I have argued above that this, too, is a mistaken assumption. Third, we would have to assume that after having formulated the cosmological doctrine, Nietzsche then chose not to incorporate it into the book for which these notes are preparatory, *The Gay Science.* He chose, instead, to incorporate only those formulations explicitly dealing with the axiological dimension of the doctrine. Why he should have suppressed material which satisfied him would be puzzling, especially to those who are familiar with Nietzsche's habits. Lastly, we would have to assume that Nietzsche was highly uncritical, that he saw no problem whatsoever in deducing an axiology from a cosmology. Since Nietzsche nowhere attempts such a "deduction," we would have to assume that Nietzsche did not see this problem at all, that his reaction is an unreflective psychological response.

To be sure, the *Nachlass* supports the view that Nietzsche regarded the doctrine of eternal recurrence as "the most scientific of all hypotheses,"[37] and further exhibits Nietzsche's view that "the law of conservation of energy demands eternal recurrence."[38] These often quoted phrases, if offered as evidence to support the logical, epistemological and/or chronological priority of the cosmological version of the doctrine of eternal recurrence, simply won't do. First, both phrases

[35] GOA *Nachlass* XII, 64: "Meine Lehre sagt: so leben, dass du wünschen musst, wieder zu leben, ist die Aufgabe – du wirst es jedenfalls!"

[36] Cf. GOA, XII.

[37] GOA *Nachlass* XV, 182: "die wissenschaftlichste aller Hypothesen."

[38] GOA *Nachlass* XVI, 398: "Der Satz vom Bestehen der Energie fordert die ewige Wiederkehr."

were written in the late eighties, were written after the cosmological and axiological versions had been recorded and after the axiological dimension had been explored in print. Second, Nietzsche's claim that the doctrine of eternal recurrence is "the most scientific" hypothesis does not necessarily imply that it is an empirical/cosmological hypothesis. The term *wissenschaftlichste* (most scientific) carries a far more restricted meaning in English than it does in German. The term "scientific" has been pre-empted, in English, by the "exact" sciences, the "natural" and "mathematical" sciences. In English the term "the most scientific" immediately suggests methodological rigor, empirical verification, or an axiomatized deductive system. However, the noun *Wissenschaft* ("science") also means "knowledge," "learning" or "scholarship." We would probably wince if the Arts and Humanities were referred to as "sciences" in ordinary English usage. Yet, the *philologisch-historische Wissenschaften* are, precisely, the "Humanities." Similarly, the adjective "scientific" has a much more restricted meaning in English than does its German "counterpart" *wissenschaftlich*. In German it suggests "scholarly," "learned," as well as "scientific." Nietzsche's assertion that the doctrine of eternal recurrence is "the most scientific" hypothesis leaves in doubt the "area" to which it belongs. No one would cringe at the suggestion that the *wissenschaftlichste* hypothesis is an axiological or metaphysical postulate – if he were Nietzsche's German contemporary. It is a feature of the English language that we do encounter considerable embarrassment when suggesting "the most scientific" axiological or metaphysical hypothesis. Since the term "the most scientific" can apply with equal force to an hypothesis in either of the two dimensions we suggested – empirical and axiological – it does not follow that Nietzsche's claim to have discovered "the most scientific" hypothesis means, specifically, an empirical postulate. Third, the opinion that the law of conservation "demands" eternal recurrence surely does not entail the *"how"* of that demand. It doesn't even *suggest* how the former "demands" the latter. Are we to understand that the cosmological entries, quoted earlier, are the explications of the "how" of that demand? Or is this simply another suggestive entry, which Nietzsche later ignored? If the former is the case, then no new light is shed on the empirical arguments. If the latter alternative is the case, again, nothing new in principle is introduced.

Nonetheless, the problem of relating the "cosmology" to the "axiology" remains. If we reject the view, as we have done, that the implications of the doctrine of eternal recurrence express Nietzsche's psychological response to an empirical cosmology, we are left with only two options. We can hunt, in vain, for evidence that Nietzsche presented 'transformation" rules which would relate the empirical to the axiological theory of eternal recurrence. We would have to find a great many premises, I am afraid; among them that all actions are reducible to energy transformations within a configuration, that all qualities are reducible to quantity transformations and, at least, that no novel quality-action-matter-energy configuration can ever emerge. There would have to be a great many more assumptions, I regret to say. If Nietzsche had inferred an axiology from his empirical formulations, he would indeed have taken quite a leap. The second alternative, for which we have been arguing all along, is to suggest that Nietzsche's cosmological argument is a consequence or corollary of, not the cause of, some more basic insight (axiological and existential). Indeed, the thought of eternal recurrence occurred to Nietzsche in August 1881 "6000 feet beyond man and time." [39] This is hardly empirical terrain. And as Nietzsche himself asserts, his published works are an attempt to articulate this insight – the doctrine of eternal recurrence: "I now relate the story of Zarathustra. The basic conception of this work (is) the eternal recurrence notion." [40] Of course, I do not suggest that Nietzsche was uninterested in finding empirical confirmation for his doctrine. On the contrary, he was very much interested in finding empirical confirmation, but apparently for a doctrine which he had embraced for reasons other than empirical cogency.

---

[39] GOA XV, *Ecce Homo*, 85: "6000 Fuss jenseits von Mensch und Zeit."
[40] GOA XV, *Ecce Homo*, 85: "Ich erzähle nunmehr die Geschichte des Zarathustra. Die Grundconception des Werkes, der Ewige-Wiederkunfts-Gedanke ..."

CHAPTER III

NIETZSCHE'S EXISTENTIAL IMPERATIVE

The twenty-four entries (numbers 90–114) concerning the empirical basis of the doctrine of eternal recurrence, found in the notes from the period of *The Gay Science,* are grouped under the heading "Presentation and Foundation of the Doctrine."[1] The remaining seventeen entries under 'The Eternal Recurrence," (numbers 115–132) are incorporated under the title "Effect of the Doctrine upon Mankind."[2] It is the problematic posed by the latter title which was explored in *The Gay Science* and subsequent works.

Nietzsche expresses the independent status of the axiological problematic succinctly: "Even if the circular repetition is only a probability or possibility, even the thought of a possibility can shatter and transform us – not only experiences or definite expectations! How the (mere) possibility of eternal damnation has worked."[3] Moreover, the two directions in which the doctrine of eternal recurrence is developed by Nietzsche are already implied in this note; the axiological and metaphysical. Within the axiological context eternal recurrence functions as a postulate eternalizing life, with the corresponding exultation or despair which such a realization would bring to the individual. Metaphysically, the doctrine of eternal recurrence functions as a revaluation of values, challenging metaphysics, Christianity, and nihilism, through the transformation of a "beyond" into an eternal "now."[4]

Nietzsche writes in his notes: "My doctrine declares: the task is to

---

[1] GOA *Nachlass* XII, 51–63.

[2] *Ibid.,* 63–69.

[3] *Ibid.,* 65: "Wenn die Kreis-Wiederholung auch nur eine Wahrscheinlichkeit oder Möglichkeit ist, auch der Gedanke einer Möglichkeit kann uns erschüttern und umgestalten, nicht nur Empfindungen oder bestimmte Erwartungen! Wie hat die Möglichkeit der ewigen Verdammnis gewirkt."

[4] The "metaphysical" dimension will be dealt with later.

live in such a way that you must wish to live again – you will *anyway*."[5] The philosophic meaning of this entry is stated in greater detail in *The Gay Science:*

> *The greatest stress:* What, if one day or night a demon were to sneak after you into your loneliest loneliness and say to you, "This life as you now live it and have lived it, you will have to live once more and innumerable times more; and there will be nothing new in it, but every pain and every joy and every thought and sigh and everything unspeakably small or great must return to you – all in the same succession and sequence – even this spider and this moonlight between the trees, and even this moment and I myself. The eternal hourglass of existence is turned over and over, and you with it, a dust grain of dust." Would you not throw yourself down and gnash your teeth and curse the demon who spoke thus? Or have you once experienced a tremendous moment when you would have answered him, "You are a god, and never have I heard anything more godly." If this thought were to gain possession of you, it would transform you, as you are, or perhaps crush you. The question regarding each and every thing, "Do you want this once more and innumerable times more?" would weigh upon your actions as the greatest stress. Or how well disposed would you have to become to yourself and to life to *crave nothing more* than this ultimate eternal confirmation and seal?[6]

When the axiological dimension of the doctrine of eternal recurrence, as cited above, is interpreted in a straightforward way, i.e., when the doctrine is interpreted in a literal fashion analogous to the interpretation of the cosmological version, severe internal inconsis-

---

[5] GOA *Nachlass* XII, 64: "Meine Lehre sagt: so leben, dass du wünschen musst, wieder zu leben, ist die Aufgabe, – du wirst es jedenfalls!"

[6] *Kleinoktavausgabe* (GOA) VI *Die Fröhliche Wissenschaft* 291–292: "Wie, wenn dir eines Tages oder Nachts ein Dämon in deine einsamste Einsamkeit nachschliche und dir sagte: 'Dieses Leben, wie du es jetzt lebst und gelebt hast, wirst du noch ein Mal und unzählige Male leben müssen; und es wird nichts Neues daran sein, sondern jeder Schmerz und jede Lust und jeder Gedanke und Seufzer und alles unsaglich Kleine und Grosse deines Lebens muss dir wiederkommen, und Alles in derselben Reihe und Folge – und ebenso diese Spinne und dieses Mondlicht zwischen den Bäumen, und ebenso dieser Augenblick und ich selber. Die ewige Sanduhr des Daseins wird immer wieder umgedreht – und du mit ihr, Stäubchen vom Staube!' Würdest du dich nicht niederwerfen und mit den Zähnen knirschen und den Dämon verfluchen, der so redete? Oder hast du einmal einen ungeheuren Augenblick erlebt, wo du ihm antworten würdest: 'du bist ein Gott und nie hörte ich Göttlicheres!' Wenn jener Gedanke über dich Gewalt bekäme, er würde dich, wie du bist, verwandeln und vielleicht zermalmen; die Frage bei Allem und Jedem: 'willst du dies noch ein Mal und noch unzählige Male?' würde als das grösste Schwergewicht auf deinem Handeln liegen! Oder wie müsstest du dir selber und dem Leben gut werden, um nach Nichts *mehr zu verlangen* als nach dieser letzten ewigen Bestätigung und Besiegelung?"

tencies arise. How is the regulative nature implied by the doctrine of eternal recurrence to be reconciled with an eternally recurring and objective identical life? If our lives are in fact but eternal repetitions, containing the same anguish, exultation and monotony, does it make sense to postulate an imperative enjoining us to live *as if* our lives recur eternally? More significantly, if our lives as now experienced are but repetitions of an infinity of lives identically endured, is there not a determinism implied in this doctrine, thus vitiating all imperatives? If the eternal recurrence expresses a "natural" law, how can it become an object of choice? It would, on the surface, seem as meaningless to exhort one to live "as if" there were an eternal recurrence as exhorting one to live "as if" subjected to the law of gravity.

On a literal level Nietzsche's doctrine of eternal recurrence poses one question not resolved by the texts: does *everything* – the logically possible as well as the historically actual, man and nature – move in an eternal cycle identical at each point within the circle? Without a satisfactory answer to this question, the doctrine of eternal recurrence seems to involve an internal cleavage. On the one hand, it functions as a descriptive hypothesis, while functioning as a regulative principle, on the other hand. The assertion that life recurs eternally (empirically) is difficult to reconcile with the exhortation to live as if it recurred eternally.

As a consequence of this ambiguity, many Nietzsche interpreters have minimized the conceptual value of the doctrine of eternal recurrence altogether. Karl Jaspers, for example, stops just short of Baeumler's and Bertram's rejection of the eternal recurrence notion by repudiating the cognitive status of the idea: "The concept as such in its empty rationality with its unmediated content . . . is for us a useless means of expressing primal experiences of man . . ."[7] The origin of the idea is not a playful intellectual reflection in Nietzsche, but the existential experience (*Seinserfahrung*) of a moment, which, in so far as it gave rise to this idea, gave this moment a decisive metaphysical meaning because of it."[8] Those who have attempted to rescue the conceptual status of the eternal recurrence doctrine against the existential-experiential thrust have been beset by the inconsistencies of the doctrine and have frequently been forced merely to impose some

---

[7] Karl Jaspers, *Nietzsche: Einführung in das Verständnis seines Philosophierens* (Berlin: De Gruyter, 1950), p. 361.

[8] *Ibid.*, p. 354.

meaning (conceptual) upon the eternal recurrence. Thus Löwith declares: "If everything returns . . . then the demand to live 'as-if' would lose all meaning. The second, the cosmological meaning, creates a fundamental contradiction . . . If human life is merely a ring within the larger ring of the eternal recurrence of all that is . . . what meaning would there be in a will to go beyond oneself, to want a European future, to will anything at all . . . On the basis of its educational character, one must understand Nietzsche's teaching as subjective, as a 'fiction,' an 'As-If' there were an objective recurrence." [9]

Although many Nietzsche scholars [10] have accepted the subjective postulatory interpretation of the eternal recurrence notion, it is difficult to understand why Nietzsche would have considered it such a momentous thought if this were the case. It is difficult to glorify a "fiction" whose psychological value is no greater than the contrary assertion: that is, by proclaiming man's radical finitude, rather than his eternal recurrence, the same consequences might follow. If I were persuaded that beyond my temporal existence nothingness awaited me, this thought too might be a "greatest stress," in so far as I could ask myself the question: do you want *this* once and *once only*? Moreover, such a postulate (finitude) might avoid the label of a "fiction."

Up to now an attempt has been made to understand the doctrine of eternal recurrence analytically, in terms of its internal consistency. Viewed from such a perspective, the doctrine is held to be either fundamentally defective, ambiguous, or inconsistent. The description of man and world as eternally recurring would appear irreconcilable with the exhortation to transform one's life. If our lives are but repetitions of the self-same, backward and forward, our lives would seem to be determined in advance.

It is possible, of course, that the analytic perspective employed in Chapter Two and now, weakens the thrust of Nietzsche's doctrine. Perhaps the most fruitful dimensions of the doctrine of eternal recurrence were bypassed by imposing an analytical context which is essen-

---

[9] *Nietzsches Philosophie der ewigen Wiederkehr des Gleichen* (Stuttgart: Kohlhammer, 1956), p. 91.

[10] Foremost among those whose general perspective Löwith shares, despite variations in emphasis, are: Georg Simmel, *Schopenhauer und Nietzsche* (Leipzig: Dunker & Humblot, 1907), Hans Vaihinger, *Die Philosophie Als-Ob* (Berlin: Reuther & Reichard, 1902), and Oscar Ewald, *Nietzsches Lehre in ihren Grundbegriffen: Die Ewige Wiederkunft des Gleichen und der Sinn des Übermenschen* (Berlin: Hofmann, 1903).

tially foreign to Nietzsche's thought. Perhaps the search for logical consistency unwittingly imposed the procrustean law of contradiction upon a thinker for whom that law, too, needs justification. It is certain that if by means of consistency we were to attempt to justify Nietzsche's doctrine *sub specie aeternitatis,* we would authenticate what Nietzsche held to be "a fable." [11] This is not to suggest that the concept of eternal recurrence is to be understood only by adopting a context of irrationality. However, if total lack of structure were the fundamental character of the totality of that-which-is, then the quest for consistency and logical validity would be derivative realities to be explained in terms of this more fundamental reality. And Nietzsche's vitriolic and unkantian critique of reason was designed, in part, to rob reason of any claim to exclusivity or autonomy. From this perspective reason is not viewed as a self-certifying judge in the court of reality, so to speak, but as a defendant on trial. Nietzsche's crusade against reason and structure retains the inherent paradox of presenting arguments against both, thereby presenting a more "reasonable" view of being.

The doctrine of eternal recurrence, then, might be profitably analyzed within the context of its opposition to three interpenetrating realities, as Nietzsche understood them: Metaphysics, Christianity, and nihilism. Since Zarathustra is the teacher of eternal recurrence, it might well be asked: at what point in history does Zarathustra emerge; against whom and what does he proclaim his teaching?

One of the most succinct and pregnant aphorisms dealing with these themes comes from the *The Twilight of the Idols.* It completes a six entry polemical vivisection of philosophy, under the title "'Reason' in Philosophy:" [12]

How the "True World" Finally Became A Fable;
history of an error
1. The true world; attainable for the sage, the pious, the virtuous one – he lives in it, *he is it.* (Oldest form of the idea, relatively clever, simple, persuasive. Circumlocution for the sentence, "I, Plato, *am* the truth.")
2. The true world; unattainable for now, but promised for the sage, the pious, the virtuous one ("for the sinner who repents") (Progress of the idea: it becomes more subtle, deceptive, incomprehensible – *it becomes female,* it becomes Christian . . .)
3. The true world; unattainable, indemonstrable, unpromisable, but the

[11] GOA VIII *Die Götzendämmerung,* 82.
[12] *Ibid.*

thought of it – a consolation, an obligation, an imperative. (The old sun at bottom, but penetrating through mist and skepticism; the idea has become elusive, pale, nordic, Königsbergian.)

4. The true world – unattainable? At any rate, unattained. And as unattained, also *unknown*. Consequently, also not consoling, redeeming, or obligating: to what could something unknown obligate us?. . . (Gray morning. First yawn of reason. Cockcrow of positivism.)

5. The "true world" – an idea which is no longer useful for anything, not even obligating – a useless idea, an idea become superfluous, *consequently,* a refuted idea; let us abolish it! (Bright day; breakfast; return of *bon sens* and cheerfulness; Plato's embarrassed blush; pandemonium of all free spirits.)

6. The true world we have abolished: Which world remained? The apparent one perhaps?. . . But no! *With the true world we have abolished the apparent one as well!* (Noon; moment of the briefest shadow; and of the longest error; high point of humanity; INCIPIT ZARATHUSTRA.) [13]

1. The "true world," as the world beyond [14] the eternal stream of becoming – *meta ta physika* – is "a fable," an "error." It is not created by Plato in the spirit of a detached formulation – detachment masks passion for Nietzsche – but as a *will* to render intelligible: "To *stamp* the character of being upon becoming – that is *the highest will-to-*

---

[13] *Ibid.* "Wie die 'wahre Welt' endlich zur Fabel wurde / Geschichte eines Irrthums / 1. Die wahre Welt, erreichbar für den Weisen, den Frommen, / den Tugendhaften – er lebt in ihr, *er ist sie.* / (Älteste Form der Idee, relativ klug, simpel / überzeugend. Umschreibung des Satzes 'ich, Plato, / bin die Wahrheit'.) / Die Wahre Welt, unerreichbar für jetzt, aber versprochen / für den Weisen, den Frommen, den Tugendhaften ('für den / Sünder, der Busse thut') / (Fortschritt der Idee: sie wird feiner, verfänglicher, unfasslicher, – *sie wird Weib,* sie wird christlich . . .) / 3. Die wahre Welt, unerreichbar, unbeweisbar, / unversprechbar, aber schon als gedacht ein Trost, / eine Verpflichtung, ein Imperativ. / (Die alte Sonne im Grunde, aber durch Nebel / und Skepsis hindurch; die Idee sublim geworden, / bleich, nordisch, königsbergisch.) / 4. Die wahre Welt – unerreichbar? Jedenfalls unerreicht. / Und als unerreicht auch *unbekannt.* Folglich auch nicht / tröstend, erlösend, verpflichtend . . . / (Grauer Morgen. Erstes Gähnen der Vernunft. / Hahnenschrei des Positivismus.) / 5. Die 'wahre Welt' – eine Idee, die zu Nichts mehr / nütz ist, nicht einmal mehr verpflichtend, – eine / unnütz, eine überflüssig gewordene Idee, / *folglich* eine widerlegte Idee: schaffen wir sie ab! / (Heller Tag; Frühstück; Rückkehr des *bon sens* / und der Heiterkeit; Schamröthe Platos; Teufelslärm / aller freien Geister.) / 6. Die wahre Welt haben wir abgeschafft: welche / Welt blieb übrig? die scheinbare vielleicht? . . . / Aber nein! *mit der wahren Welt haben wir auch / die scheinbare abgeschafft!* (Mittag; Augenblick des kürzesten Schattens; / Ende des längsten Irrthums; Höhepunkt / der Menschheit; INCIPIT ZARATHUSTRA.)"

[14] *Ibid.* Cf. also GOA VI *Also Sprach Zarathustra.* "Von den Hinterweltlern" 46–49; "Von der Selbst-Überwindung" 165–170.

power.[15] The will to truth, as the will-to-power, expresses man's spiritual domination over the world and over himself. Order is *imposed* upon the fluctuating carnival-masks of the phenomenal realm as the turbulent passions of the individual are overcome. Hence, metaphysics – which is Platonism at bottom for Nietzsche – employs "reason" as a weapon to overpower the eternal cycle of genesis, growth, decay, and death – becoming. In so far as reason cannot grasp change without turning it into a static form of being, all philosophic systems are grounded in error: "The ultimate truth about the flow of things cannot be absorbed; our organs (for life) are oriented towards error."[16] Finally, the will to know, to render intelligible, moves in two directions simultaneously. It transforms becoming into being, and being, is *my* being: "I, Plato, *am* the truth."[17] Being is my self-overcoming.

2. The wedding of Plato to Christianity, mirrored in the second stage of the aphorism, pushes the "beyond" from the "attainable" to the "promised." While the Platonic dialectic posed the ascent from the defective mode of being to the plenary mode as a task for the individual, to be accomplished in this life, Christianity suspends earthly self-overcoming altogether, from Nietzsche's point of vantage. In place of the "I am" which the true world poses as a possibility for the individual, Christianity substitutes the promise of eternity "for the sinner who repents."[18] The will to a "beyond" moves from the individual to the collective; from metaphysics to religion.

3. In Kant's critical philosophy, stage # 3, both attainment and promise of the true world are abolished. The lost "true world" is revived as a pale echo, however, in the postulates of God, freedom, and immortality. It is "the old sun" seen through the limits of reason, skepticism. The true, timeless, and eternal is no longer guaranteed by reason nor by faith, but by heeding the categorical imperative. The true world is the indemonstrable reward for consistency in conduct.

4. What is indemonstrable, unattainable, unpromisable is also unknown. Hence, the unknown can have no effect upon life in so far as it cannot address itself to consciousness. Surely, a silent voice utters

[15] GOA *Nachlass* XVI, 101: "Dem Werden den Charakter des Seins aufzuprägen – das ist der *höchste Wille zur Macht*."

[16] GOA *Nachlass* XII, 48: "Die letzte Wahrheit vom Fluss der Dinge verträgt die Einverleibung nicht, unsere Organe (zum Leben) sind auf den Irrtum eingerichtet."

[17] GOA VIII *Die Götzendämmerung*, 82.

[18] *Ibid.*

no imperative – it *is* silent. If it exists at all, then, "the true world" is wholly other, entirely beyond human communication. If only the knowable is real, how can the unknown obligate us? Stage # 4 – rise of positivism.

5. But if being – the true world – is unknown *and* indemonstrable, it is also unknowable. "Let us abolish it." [19] It is a useless idea: God is dead.

These first five historical stages, impressionistically drawn by Nietzsche in *The Twilight of Idols,* represent a history of the devaluation of values. The highest values, God, the Absolute, the timeless and eternal – indeed truth itself – have ceased to hold sway over the individual. Despite his polemical opposition to traditional metaphysics, Nietzsche did not regard this historical devaluation either as complete or as a source of unequivocal joy. For, "with the true world we have abolished the apparent one as well." [20]

Nietzsche consistently identified the dominant theme in Western thought with Platonic-Christian "otherworldliness." However, the mere historically perceived devaluation of being does not spell man's redemption in *this* world either. A distinction between appearance and reality, becoming and being, illusion and truth, can be drawn only when both elements are present in the dialectic. Without reality-being-truth, appearance-becoming-illusion do not exist as what they are either. When the "true world" sinks into oblivion, the "apparent" one ceases to exist *qua* apparent world as well. All that is left after the abolition of the true world is an aimless becoming in which all meaningful distinctions between veridical and delusory disappear. Indeed, the very possibility of meaningful criteriological distinctions becomes moot with the dissimulation of "the true world." Nietzsche characterized this aimless relativity which he experienced in every sphere of reality – cultural, political, historical, and philosophical – as nihilism. When the highest values become devalued, nihilism emerges. But the highest values become devalued not in the sense that man knowingly confronts an eternal abyss in fear and trembling. The highest values simply no longer exist. And man accepts this event not with stoic resignation but in total unawareness. Nietzsche's most forceful statement of this view follows:

[19] *Ibid.*
[20] *Ibid.*

The Madman. Have you not heard of that madman who lit a lantern in the bright morning, ran to the market place, and cried incessantly, "I seek God! I seek God!" Since many of those who were standing around just then did not believe in God, he provoked much laughter. Did he get lost? said one. Did he lose his way like a child? said another. Or is he hiding? Is he afraid of us? Has he gone on a voyage? or emigrated? – Thus they yelled and laughed all together. The madman jumped into their midst and pierced them with his glances. "Whither is God" he cried. " I shall tell you. *We have killed him* – you and I. We are his murderers. But how have we done this! How were we able to drink up the sea? Who gave us the sponge to wipe away the entire horizon? What did we do when we unchained this earth from its sun? Whither is it moving now? Whither are we moving? Away from all suns? Are we not plunging continually? Backward, sideward, forward, to all sides? Is there still an up or down? Are we not straying as through an infinite void? Does not the breath of empty space press upon us? Has it not become colder? Is not night and more night coming on constantly? Must not lanterns be lit in the morning? Do we not hear anything yet of the noise of the gravediggers who are burying God? Do we not smell anything yet of the godly decomposition? Gods too decompose. God is dead! God remains dead! And we have killed him! How shall we comfort ourselves, the murderers of all murderers? What was holiest and most powerful of all that the world hitherto possessed has bled to death under our knives. – Who will wipe this blood from us? With what water can we cleanse ourselves? What festivals of atonement, what sacred games shall we have to invent? Is not the greatness of this deed too great for us? Must not we ourselves become gods simply to seem worthy of it? There has never been a greater deed – and whoever will be born after us, for the sake of this deed he will belong to a higher history than all history hitherto." Here the madman fell silent and looked again at his listeners: they too were silent and stared at him strangely. At last he threw his lantern on the ground and it broke and went out. "I come too early," he said then, "my time has not yet come. This tremendous event is still on its way, still wandering – it has not yet pressed upon the ears of man. Lightning and thunder require time, the light of the stars requires time, deeds require time even after they are done in order to be seen and heard. This deed is still more distant from them than the most distant stars – *and yet they have done this themselves . . .*"[21]

[21] GOA VI *Die Fröhliche Wissenschaft,* 189–190: *"Der tolle Mensch:* Habt ihr nicht von jenem tollen Menschen gehört, der am hellen Vormittag eine Laterne anzündete, auf den Markt lief und unaufhörlich schrie: 'Ich suche Gott! Ich suche Gott!' – Da gerade dort viele von denen zusammen standen, welche nicht an Gott glaubten, so erregte er ein grosses Gelächter. Ist er denn verloren gegangen? sagte der Eine. Hat er sich verlaufen wie ein Kind? sagte der andere. Oder hält er sich versteckt? Fürchtet er sich vor uns? Ist er zu Schiff gegangen? ausgewandert? – so schrieen und lachten sie durcheinander. Der tolle Mensch sprang mitten unter sie und durchbohrte sie mit seinen Blicken. 'Wohin ist Gott? rief er, ich will es euch sagen! Wir haben ihn getödtet – ihr und ich! Wir alle

Zarathustra's (Nietzsche's) final task, then, is the confrontation with nihilism. And it should be noted that this is not a nihilism which proclaims the meaninglessness of a blind and mute universe. This nihilism has an anesthetic essence: it is the unreflective nihilism exhibited in daily "bon sens" and "cheerfulness" after the death of God. It is life without depth.

However, Nietzsche cannot return to a "true world" either. His own philosophic development bars this possibility. He had passed through the first two of his three celebrated stages; the three metamorphoses – camel, lion, and child.[22] The lion can no longer be a camel.

As a young philologist Nietzsche had succumbed to traditional metaphysics, in the sense that he had assumed the context and burden of seeking release from the vicissitudes of what was held to be a chimerical phenomenal world. In *The Birth of Tragedy*,[23] release from a painful existence was partially sought through an ordering principle;

---

sind seine Mörder! Aber wie haben wir dies gemacht? Wie vermochten wir das Meer auszutrinken? Wer gab uns den Schwamm, um den ganzen Horizont wegzuwischen? Wat thaten wir, als wir diese Erde von ihrer Sonne losketteten? Wohin bewegt sie sich nun? Wohin bewegen wir uns? Fort von allen Sonnen? Stürzen wir nicht fortwährend? Und rückwärts, seitwärts, vorwärts, nach allen Seiten? Giebt es noch ein Oben und ein Unten? Irren wir nich durch ein unendliches Nichts? Haucht uns nicht der leere Raum an? Ist es nicht kälter geworden? Kommt nicht immerfort die Nacht und mehr Nacht? Müssen nicht Laternen am frühen Vormittage angezündet werden? Hören wir noch nichts von dem Lärm der Todtengräber, welche Gott begraben? Riechen wir noch nichts von der Göttlichen Verwesung? – auch Götter verwesen! Gott ist todt! Gott bleibt todt! Und wir haben ihn getödtet! Wie trösten wir uns, die Mörder aller Mörder? Das Heiligste und Mächtigste, was die Welt bisher besass, es ist unter unsern Messern verblutet – wer wischt dies Blut von uns ab? Mit welchem Wasser könnten wir uns reinigen? Welche Sühnenfeiern, welche heilige Spiele werden wir erfinden müssen? Ist nicht die Grösse dieser That zu gross für uns? Müssen wir nicht selber zu Göttern werden, um nur ihrer würdig zu erscheinen? Es gab nie eine grössere That – und wer nur immer nach uns geboren wird, gehört um dieser That willen in eine höhere Geschichte, als alle Geschichte bisher war! – Hier schwieg der tolle Mensch und sah wieder seine Zuhörer an: – auch sie schwiegen und blickten befremdet auf ihn. Endlich warf er seine Laterne auf den Boden, dass sie in Stücke brach und erlosch, 'Ich komme zu früh, sagte er dann, ich bin noch nicht an der Zeit. Dies ungeheure Ereigniss ist noch unterwegs und wandert – es ist noch nicht bis zu den Ohren der Menschen gedrungen. Blitz und Donner brauchen Zeit, das Licht der Gestirne braucht Zeit, Thaten brauchen Zeit, auch nach dem sie gethan sind, um gesehen und gehört zu werden. Diese That ist ihnen immer noch ferner als die fernsten Gestirne – *und doch haben sie dieselbe gethan!* . . ."

[22] GOA VI *Also Sprach Zarathustra*, "Von den drei Verwandlungen" 33–37.
[23] GOA I.

Apollo. But Nietzsche's polemical rejection of traditional metaphysics and contexts, evident after *The Birth of Tragedy,* is in itself no affirmation. The lion's proud self-affirmation is still bound in opposition to the burden it had once assumed. In consequence, the essence of this metamorphosis is negation, rage, destruction. The eternal recurrence, on the other hand, helped Nietzsche to see the world anew and affirm it; achieve the pristine innocence of the child joyfully embracing existence. Nietzsche experienced the apotheosis of life "6,000 feet beyond man and time."[24]

To overcome the purposelessness of becoming, Nietzsche returned to his constant star, Heraclitus, and affirmed the intrinsic meaningfulness of the eternal river: "it is Heraclitus in whose company I feel better, more cheerful than anywhere else . . ."[25] The doctrine of eternal recurrence, that is, of the unconditioned and infinitely repeated circularity of all things . . . this doctrine of Zarathustra's could in the final analysis already have been taught by Heraclitus. At a minimum there are traces of it in the Stoics, who inherited almost all of their fundamental ideas from Heraclitus."[26]

Since Nietzsche tended to view metaphysics as Platonism and the history of Western man as an unholy alliance of Platonic-Christian "otherworldliness," the corrective may have been suggested, in part, by Heraclitus and the Stoics. Specifically, the influence of Heraclitus and the Stoics upon Nietzsche's formulation of the doctrine of eternal recurrence involves (at least) four shared principles: (1) monism, (2) determinism, (3) dialectical unity of opposites through strife, (4) cyclicalism. I hasten to add that the term "influence" is not being used in a mechanical causal sense here. There is no evidence that Nietzsche's doctrine of eternal recurrence was influenced by Heraclitus and the Stoics in the sense that Nietzsche discovered the doctrine there and elaborated it to suit his own purposes. Where Nietzsche speaks of his doctrine, in *Ecce Homo,* he merely scans the history of philosophy to establish his own genealogy. The concept of eternal recurrence, as

[24] GOA XV *Ecce Homo,* 85: "6000 Fuss jenseits von Mensch und Zeit."
[25] GOA *Nachlass* XII, 239: "Heraklit, in dessen Nähe mir wärmer, mir wohler zumute wird als irgendwo sonst . . ."
[26] XV *Ecce Homo,* 65: "Die Lehre von der 'ewigen Wiederkunft,' das heisst vom unbedingten und unendlich wiederholten Kreislauf aller Dinge . . . diese Lehre Zarathustras könnte zuletzt auch schon von Heraklit gelehrt worden sein. Zum mindistens hat die Stoa, die fast alle ihre grundsätzlichen Vorstellungen von Heraklit geerbt hat, Spuren davon."

we have already seen, "came" to Nietzsche like a flash in 1881. The term "influence" here is used in the restricted sense of being a contributory cause. As a classical philologist, Nietzsche was thoroughly familiar with Heraclitus and the Stoics, and their teachings probably affected the context and moment of discovery. It should also be noted, parenthetically, that we are not here concerned with demonstrating those principles which are specifically Heraclitean as opposed to those which were added by commentators. Thus, for example, the fourth above-mentioned principle – the cyclical interpretation of the cosmos – which Diogenes Laertius attributes to Heraclitus,[27] was not explicitly taught by Heraclitus. But it is in the Stoic interpretation of Heraclitus that Nietzsche finds his precursors: "this doctrine of Zarathustra's could in the final analysis already have been taught by Heraclitus. At a minimum there are traces of it in the Stoics, who inherited almost all of their fundamental ideas from Heraclitus."[28]

The four principles suggested above which Nietzsche inherited can be exhibited by briefly presenting relevant elements of Heraclitus' philosophy and the interpretation of the Stoics. To this task we now must turn.

The underlying "substance" of the cosmos is regarded by Heraclitus as fire: "This order, the same for all things, no one of gods or men has made, but it always was, and is, and ever shall be, an ever-living fire, kindling according to fixed measure, and extinguishing according to fixed measure."[29] Fire, uncreated and eternal, is the infinite and ultimate "stuff" of which the cosmos consists. Fire seems to be both active and passive; consuming, flickering, and transforming, on the one hand, while retaining an apparent identity and permanence of its own. The one substance, fire, is not a supersensuous principle lying behind the world of appearance, but is, rather, immanent: "All things are exchanged for fire, and fire for all things; as wares are exchanged

---

[27] *Diogenes Laertius*, Bk. 4, 9, 8–12 in Milton C. Nahm, *Selections from Early Greek Philosophy* (New York: Appleton-Century-Crofts, 1934), p. 96.

[28] GOA *Nachlass*, XV, *Ecce Homo*, 65.

[29] Milton C. Nahm, *Selections from Early Greek Philosophy* (New York: Appleton-Century-Crofts, 1934), p. 90. Cf. G. S. Kirk and J. E. Raven, *The Presocratic Philosophers* (Cambridge University Press, 1960), p. 199: "This world order (the same of all) did none of gods or men make, but it always was and is and shall be: an everlasting fire, kindling in measures and going out in measures."

for gold and gold for wares." [30] The process of the transformation of fire proceeds from the condensation of the sun's fire into water, and the subsequent transformation of water into earth and the "lightening flash:" "The transformations of fire are, first of all, sea; and of the sea one half is earth, and one half is lightening flash." [31] The process of condensation from sun-fire into water, and water into earth is the "downward way," while a corresponding "upward way" is simultaneously active – the liquefaction of earth into water, water into vapor, and vapor into fire. One interesting feature of Heraclitus' doctrine is that these two apparently opposed transformations, upward and downward, are conceived as fundamentally one: "Upward, downward, the way is one and the same." [32] The identity of opposites, of logical contraries, recurs in Heraclitus: "Opposition unites. From what draws apart results the most beautiful harmony. All things take place by strife." [33] "Men do not understand how that which draws apart agrees with itself; harmony lies in the bending back, as for instance of the bow and of the lyre." [34] The cosmos is One, and all apparent discreetness is but a moment of the self-transformation of the Unity into what appears as diversity: "Thou shouldst unite things whole and things not whole, that which tends to unite and that which tends to separate, the harmonious and the discordant; from all things arises the one, and from the one all things." [35] It is this organic conception of the cosmos, that diversity (in the sense of discreetness) is but an aspect of unity, which leads to assertions that, on the surface, appear contradictory: "Good and bad are the same." [36] "Life and death, and working and sleeping, and youth and old age, are the same: for the latter change and are the former, and the former change back to the latter." [37] "Gods are mortals, men are immortals, each living in the others' death and dying in the others' life." [38] Apparent paradoxes such as these, which helped to earn Heraclitus the title of "the obscure," undoubtedly fascinated Nietzsche. The demand for formal

[30] Milton C. Nahm, *Selections from Early Greek Philosophy* (New York: Appleton-Century-Crofts, 1934), p. 90.
[31] *Ibid.*, fragment 21, p. 90.
[32] *Ibid.*, fragment 69, p. 92.
[33] *Ibid.*, fragment 46, p. 91.
[34] *Ibid.*, fragment 45, p. 91.
[35] *Ibid.*, fragment 59, p. 92.
[36] *Ibid.*, fragment 57, p. 92.
[37] *Ibid.*, fragment 78, p. 93.
[38] *Ibid.*, fragment 67, p. 92.

consistency was, for Nietzsche, at best a "Platonic" derivative mode of reality. The priority of change, becoming, as an organic self-transformation appealed to Nietzsche. Change is the ultimately real. "You could not step twice in the same rivers; for other and yet other waters are ever flowing on." [39] "In the same rivers we step and we do not step; we are and we are not." [40] The affirmation of change as ultimately real also entailed for Heraclitus, as indeed it did for Nietzsche, a "law" of transformation. Natural changes are regular and harmonious, and this regularity is the *Logos*. Things, qualities, relations, events, situations, are but "moments" in a stream of structured change. The structure is the *Logos*. It should also be noted that we are *not* dealing with four different entities: (1) fire as the cosmic principle, (2) particulars as transformations of fire, (3) the *Logos* as the law of that transformation and, (4) particulars as concrete expressions of that *Logos*. For Heraclitus all four are one. There is no "universal" fire which is not at the same time the self-transforming particular; no *Logos* which is not identical with its particular expression: "God is day and night, winter and summer, war and peace, satiety and hunger; but he assumes different forms, just as when incense is mingled with incense; everyone gives him the name he pleases." [41]

It would appear that human behavior is also governed by the *Logos:* "For they are absolutely destined . . ." [42] "Man, like a light in the night, is kindled and put out." [43] As an expression of the cosmic principle, the soul is kindled and extinguished. Thus the metaphors of light, fire, and heat here emerge in relation to the soul as well: "The dry soul is wisest and best. A dry beam in the wisest and best soul. Where the earth is dry, the soul is wisest and best." [44] The most illumined (dryest) soul is the soul most like the cosmic principle; fire. "For to souls it is death to become water, and for water it is death to become earth; but water is formed from earth, and from water, soul." [45] This fragment ties together the "physical" and "behavioral" aspects of being. The fire-water-earth evolutions are the upward-downward way (the *logos*) of the One: Fire. The soul, too, is a part of

---

[39] *Ibid.,* fragments 41–42, p. 91.
[40] *Ibid.,* fragment 81, p. 93.
[41] *Ibid.,* fragment 36, p. 91.
[42] *Ibid.,* fragment 63, p. 92.
[43] *Ibid.,* fragment 77, p. 93.
[44] *Ibid.,* fragments 74–76, p. 93.
[45] *Ibid.,* fragment 68, p. 92.

this cosmic process, and it is death for it "to become water." It is wise when "dry." Yet, interestingly, Heraclitus says: "It is a delight to souls to become wet."[46] This fragment is not designed to contradict the previously quoted fragment. On the contrary. It suggests that the soul's *tendency* is toward folly: "Whenever a man gets drunk, he is led about by a beardless boy, stumbling, not knowing whither he goes, for his soul is wet."[47] The multitude is apparently ignorant and in its ignorance its soul is dying: "Those who hear without the power to understand are like deaf men; the proverb holds true of them – 'Present, they are absent.'"[48]

Heraclitus' assertion of the primacy and "lawfulness" of becoming, and the implication that man, too, is a part of the eternal stream and thus equally a child of cosmic forces, no doubt affected Nietzsche's thinking. But he was equally impressed with Heraclitus' acceptance of the testimony of our senses: "What can be seen, heard and learned, this I prize."[49] Nietzsche's own attitude toward Heraclitus, outside of the context of the eternal recurrence doctrine, was made explicit in *The Twilight of the Idols*:

With the highest respect I accept the name of *Heraclitus*. When the rest of the philosophic folk rejected the testimony of the senses because they showed multiplicity and change, he rejected their testimony because they showed things as if they had permanence and unity. Heraclitus too did the senses an injustice. They lie neither in the way the Eleatics believed, nor as he believed – they do not lie at all. What we *make* of their testimony, that alone introduces lies; for example, the lie of unity, the lie of thinghood, of substance, of permanence. "Reason" is the cause of our falsification of the testimony of the senses. Insofar as the senses show becoming, passing away, and change, they do not lie. But Heraclitus will remain eternally right with his assertion that being is an empty fiction. The "apparent" world is the only one: the "true" world is merely *added by a lie.*[50]

---

[46] *Ibid.*, fragment 72, p. 92.
[47] *Ibid.*, fragment 73, p. 92–93.
[48] *Ibid.*, fragment 3, p. 89.
[49] *Ibid.*, fragment 13, p. 89.
[50] GOA VIII, *Die Götzendämmerung*, 78: "Ich nehme mit hoher Ehrerbietung, den Namen *Heraklits* beiseite. Wenn das andre Philosophen-Volk das Zeugnis der Sinne verwarf, weil dieselben Vielheit und Veränderung zeigten, verwarf er deren Zeugnis, weil sie die Dinge zeigten, als ob sie Dauer und Einheit hätten. Auch Heraklit tat den Sinnen unrecht. Dieselben lügen weder in der Art, wie die Eleaten es glaubten, noch wie er es glaubte – sie lügen überhaupt nicht. Was wir aus ihrem Zeugnis *machen,* das legt erst die Lüge hinein, zum Beispiel die Lüge der Einheit, die Lüge der Dinglichkeit, der Substanz, der

It would appear, then, that Nietzsche's primary conscious debt to Heraclitus involves the affirmation of change as the real, the unqualified rejection of being – the "true world." However, Nietzsche also asserted that the doctrine of eternal recurrence *could* have been taught by Heraclitus and that traces of this doctrine are present in the Stoics.

It is true that Heraclitus *could* have taught such a doctrine, although he did not do so explicitly. His commentators and Stoic heirs certainly thought that he had taught something like a doctrine of eternal recurrence. Diogenes Laertius, in attributing a doctrine of eternal recurrence to Heraclitus, summarized his teachings as follows:

> Coming to his particular tenets, we may state them as follows: fire is the element, all things are exchange for fire and come into being by rarefaction and condensation; but of this he gives no clear explanation. All things come into being by conflict of opposites, and the sum of things flows like a stream. Further, all that is is limited and forms one world. And it is alternately born from fire and again resolved into fire in fixed cycles to all eternity, and this is determined by destiny.[51]

The doctrine of eternal recurrence, or some version thereof, plays a more explicit role in Stoic thought than in Heraclitus. Nietzsche's contention that traces of the doctrine are present in the Stoa is historically correct. For example, Aristocles ascribes to Zeno of Citium the following view:

> Zeno said the fundamental substance of all existing things is fire, in this following Heraclitus, and the principles of fire, he said, were matter and God, here following Plato. But he asserted that they both were bodies, an active and a passive, whereas Plato said that the primary active cause was incorporeal. Next, the whole cosmos at certain fated periods is dissolved by fire, and then again formed into a world. Now the primary fire is like a kind of seed, containing the "reasons" of all things and the causes of everything, past, present, and future. Now the union and sequence of these things is an inevitable and unavoidable fate, knowledge, truth, and the law of existing things.[52]

Dauer ... Die 'Vernunft' ist die Ursache, dass wir das Zeugnis der Sinne fälschen. Sofern die Sinne das Werden, das Vergehen, den Wechsel zeigen, lügen sie nicht ... Aber damit wird Heraklit ewig recht behalten, dass das Sein eine leere Fiktion ist. Die 'scheinbare' Welt ist die einzige: die 'wahre Welt' ist nur *hinzugelogen*."

[51] Milton C. Nahm, *Selections from Early Greek Philosophy* (New York: Appleton-Century-Crofts, 1934) fragment 130b, p. 96.

[52] Gordon H. Clark, *Selections from Hellenistic Philosophy* (New York: Appleton-Century-Crofts, 1940), p. 68.

Here, certainly, "traces" of the doctrine are explicitly present. But we also find that the Stoics, more explicitly than Heraclitus, concern themselves with the problem of human conduct, in the light of the doctrine of eternal recurrence. Since the Stoic cosmology did assume "an unending series of world-constructions and world-destructions,"[53] the implications of this doctrine regarding human freedom were never evaded by them.

Consistently with this belief the Stoics denied human freedom, or rather liberty for them meant doing consciously, with assent, what one will do in any case . . . This reign of necessity the Stoics expressed under the concept of Fate, but Fate is not something different from God and universal reason, nor is it different from Providence which orders all things for the best. Fate and Providence are but different aspects of God. But this cosmological determinism is modified by their insistence on interior freedom, in the sense that a man can alter his judgment and his attitude towards events, seeing them and welcoming them as expressions of "God's will."[54]

It would, of course, be tempting to suggest that Nietzsche adopted the doctrine of eternal recurrence as a cosmology and axiological principle on the basis of his familiarity with Heraclitus and Stoic sources. But any such interpretation would have to come to grips with Nietzsche's assertion that he found only "traces" of the doctrine in Stoic sources. What then, are those traces? What Nietzsche discovered in his Stoic precursors was, on the one hand, an explicitly cyclical cosmology and, on the other hand, the problem of determinism as regards human action. Beyond that point important differences emerge, as will later be shown.

Perhaps the most significant question raised by Nietzsche's awareness of the genealogy of the doctrine of eternal recurrence is this: Was he also aware of the fact that the Stoics had explored the relationship between the cosmology and axiology? This is an important question in several respects. Nietzsche commentators have, on the whole, found it difficult to reconcile the cosmology of eternal recurrence with the axiology of eternal recurrence. They have generally suggested an incompatibility of the two, or that the axiology is a subjective "fiction" or else a psychological reaction. However, one finds the same conceptual difficulty in Stoic thought. Yet Stoic philosophers were aware of some of the difficulties and proceeded to suggest resolutions

[53] Frederick Copleston, S. J., *A History of Philosophy*, vol. I (London: Burns and Oates Ltd., 1966), p. 389.
[54] *Ibid.*, p. 389.

(whether satisfactory or not is not at issue). It would be extremely odd for Nietzsche to assert, on the one hand, that traces of his doctrine are present in Stoic thought while, on the other hand, remaining ignorant of the fact that the doctrine there posed difficulties which demanded and received attention. In fact, Nietzsche's awareness of the genealogy of the doctrine of eternal recurrence may serve as additional evidence to support the thesis that the axiology of eternal recurrence is at least as important as the cosmology, in so far as the Stoics themselves recognized the importance of this dimension. One finds it difficult to imagine that Nietzsche, familiar with Stoic writings as he was, found only "cosmological" traces of the doctrine of eternal recurrence, claiming *amor fati* as his own exclusive insight, while ignoring difficulties raised by the relationship between a cyclical cosmology and axiology.

The relationship between "necessity," "fate," "principal causes" and "auxiliary and proximate causes" occupies an important place in Stoic writings. Quotations such as the two which follow, either attacking or explicating the above-mentioned concepts, are a part of Stoic thought or a commentary upon it which did not escape Nietzsche's attention. Alexander Aphrodisias, in commenting on the fact that "fate" does not imply "necessity," suggests a distinction:

one may say also, the proposition "there will be a naval battle tomorrow" can be true, but cannot also be necessary. For the necessary is always true, and this will no longer remain true after the battle occurs. But if this is not necessary, neither does the thing signified by the proposition, there will be a battle, occur of necessity. But if it is to be, though not of necessity (for that there will be a battle is true but not necessary) it is obviously possible. And if possible, the possible is not ruled out by the fact that everything occurs by fate.[55]

This extremely rich observation approaches the empirical problem posed by the doctrine of fate by raising an epistemological distinction. Although empirical propositions may be true ("there will be a battle tomorrow") they are not necessarily true. By anticipating later epistemological distinctions, this remark distinguishes analytic and synthetis propositions in such a way that empirical propositions are possible (synthetic) and not necessary (analytic). Hence, Alexander Aphrodisias concludes that possibility, contingency, is not ruled out by Stoic cosmological fatalism.

[55] Gordon H. Clark, *Selections from Hellenistic Philosophy* (New York: Appleton-Century-Crofts, 1940), p. 101.

Cicero typically comments quite directly on the possibility of raising a distinction between fate and necessity, and on the history of that problem. It is worth quoting at length, I think.

It seems to me that the ancient philosophers were of two opinions, one group holding that fate so controls everything that it exerts the force of necessity, ... the other group holding that the voluntary motions of the soul occur without any influence of fate. Chrysippus, however, wished to hold a middle course like an honorary arbiter, but he rather attaches himself to those who believed that the motions of the soul are free from necessity. But by the expression he uses, he falls back into the same difficulties so that unwillingly he affirms the necessity of fate. Let us see, therefore, how this affects assent. Those ancient philosophers, for whom everything occurs by fate, say that assent is produced by force and necessity. The others, however, who disagree, free assent from fate and assert that if fate rules assent, necessity cannot be avoided ... But Chrysippus, since he both rejects necessity and does not wish anything to happen without preceding causes, distinguishes two kinds of causes, so that he may escape necessity and retain fate. "For," he says, "perfect and principal causes are one thing, auxiliary and proximate causes are another. For which reason, when we say everything happens by fate and antecedent causes, we do not mean perfect and principal causes, but auxiliary and proximate." And so, the position I argued above, he opposes as follows: "If everything happens by fate, of course it follows that everything happens by preceding causes, but they are not principal and perfect; they are auxiliary and proximate. And if these are not in our power, it does not follow that our appetites are not in our power. But this would follow if we should say everything happens by perfect and principal causes, so that when these causes are not in our power, our appetites are not in our power. For which reason those who introduce fate as to join necessity with it, must accept that conclusion; but those who do not say that antecedent causes must be perfect and principal escape that conclusion.[56]

Whether Cicero's interpretation of Chrysippus' position regarding principal and proximate causes is correct is not at issue here. It is a fact, however, that historians of philosophy generally agree that the Stoic ethic is not, strictly speaking, deterministic, in the sense that they generally held that one's attitude toward fate was a matter of chief concern for the individual and subject to modification. Windelband states the matter as follows:

The leading power, or governing part of the soul, is, for them, not only that which makes perceptions out of the excitations of the individual organs in sensation, but also that by which its assent transforms excitations of the feelings into activities of the will. This consciousness, whose voca-

[56] *Ibid.,* pp. 101–102.

tion is to apprehend and form its content as a unity, is, according to its proper and true nature, reason (*nous*); the states, therefore, in which consciousness allows itself to be hurried along to assent by the violence of excitement contradicts, in like measure, its own nature and reason. These states (*affectus*) are, then, those of passion and disease of the soul; they are perturbations of the soul, contrary to Nature and contrary to reason. Hence the wise man, if he cannot defend himself from those excitations of feeling in presence of the world, will deny them his assent with the power of reason; he does not allow them to become passions or emotions, his virtue is the *absence of emotions (apatheia)*. His overcoming of the world is his overcoming of his own impulses. It is not until we give our assent that we become dependent upon the course of things; if we withhold it, our personality remains immovable, resting upon itself. If man cannot hinder fate from preparing for him pleasure and pain, he may, nevertheless, by esteeming the former as not a good, and the latter as not an evil, keep the proud consciousness of his self-sufficiency. Hence, in itself, virtue is for the Stoics the sole good, and on the other hand, vice, which consists in the control of the reason by the passions, is the sole evil.[57]

It is this type of Stoic formulation (that although human action is part and parecl of a natural order, cyclical and determined, it is nonetheless within our powers to modify those determining forces) which is supposed to answer the question of how moral action is possible.

We maintained earlier, without support, that Nietzsche was well aware of the difficulty Stoic philosophers encountered in maintaining a deterministic cosmology while, simultaneously, asserting ethical imperatives. Fortunately, this claim is not a matter of speculation. Nietzsche, ironically, was unimpressed by the *logic* of the Stoic injunction that one ought to "live according to Nature," precisely on the grounds that it is *impossible* to do otherwise – given Stoic "fatalism:" "And granting your imperative 'live according to Nature,' at bottom it means the same as 'live according to Life' – how could you *not* do it? Why make a principle of that which you yourself are and must be?"[58] Whether Nietzsche's judgment is adequate to the distinctions Stoic philosophers previously introduced is not important. What is

---

[57] Wilhelm Windelband, *A History of Philosophy*, vol. I (Harper Torchbook: Harper and Row, 1958), p. 168.

[58] Karl Schlechta, editor, *Werke in Drei Bänden* (Carl Hanser Verlag: München, 1955), vol. II, "Jenseits von Gut und Böse," p. 573: "Und gesetzt, euer Imperativ 'gemäss der Natur leben' bedeutet im Grunde so viel als 'gemäss dem Leben leben' – wie könntet ihr's denn *nicht*? Wozu ein Prinzip aus dem Machen, was ihr selbst seid und sein müsst?"

relevant here is that Nietzsche correctly diagnosed a logical problem in Stoic thought, and objected to their resolution of it. It is, of course, ironic that the same problem plagues our treatment of Nietzsche's doctrine of eternal recurrence. Having objected to the Stoic canon to "live according to Nature," on the grounds that it cannot be an imperative at all since it is impossible to "violate" it, the duality of Nietzsche's own doctrine of eternal recurrence seems to retain the same inconsistency. It is, of course, possible that Nietzsche failed to recognize that his objections to the Stoic imperative could also count as a self-indictment. If Nietzsche exhorts us to live in such a way that we must wish to live again, the additional declaration – that we will anyway – seems to introduce an insuperable difficulty.

Without directly confronting that problem at this point, it may be well to summarize the possible influences of Heraclitus and the Stoics upon Nietzsche's formulation of the doctrine of eternal recurrence, in the light of the preceding discussion.

First and foremost, the Stoics clearly taught a cyclical cosmology, thus vindicating Nietzsche's claim that "traces" of the doctrine of eternal recurrence are to be found there. His further claim, that the doctrine could have been taught by Heraclitus as well, is justified to the extent that Heraclitus' commentators ascribe a cyclical cosmology to him. Second, the anti-dualistic emphasis in Heraclitus and the Stoics finds its counterpart in Nietzsche's eternal recurrence doctrine. Third, Heraclitus' affirmation of becoming, change, as the ultimate reality is a conviction shared by Nietzsche. Fourth, the Stoic recognition that a cyclical and fatalistic cosmology poses problems for a corresponding axiology was clear to Nietzsche as well.

Significantly, I believe, Nietzsche rejected the Stoic resolution of the implication of the doctrine of eternal recurrence without reservation. In fact, he rejected it in a polemical manner usually reserved for his barbs against Platonism and Christianity:

Your pride wants to prescribe and incorporate into Nature, even Nature, your Morality, your ideal; you demand that Nature be "according to the Stoa," and want to create all existence only according to your own image – as an enormous eternal glorification and universalization of Stoicism! With all your love of truth you force yourselves for so long, so tenaciously, so hypnotically rigid, to see Nature *falsely,* namely stoically, until you are no longer capable of seeing it in any other way.[59]

[59] *Ibid.,* p. 573: "Euer Stolz will der Natur, sogar der Natur, eure Moral, eure Ideal vorschreiben und einverleiben, ihr verlangt, dass sie 'der Stoa gemäss'

Nietzsche's objection to the Stoic ethic, that it falsifies nature, also reflects his general opposition to the ideal of the sage, and his aversion to what he considered a Platonic disease, namely, the creation of two realms only one of which was "legitimate." The flight from the realm of becoming, from which Platonic metaphysics allegedly seeks release is, for Nietzsche, a flight from the senses, pain, deception, and passion. Hence the Stoic ethic, with its ideal of the sage, is but another moral Platonism for Nietzsche – despite its cyclical fatalism. To the extent that the Stoic ethic opposes passion, it is symptomatic of what Nietzsche was fond of calling the decline of life:

> How the preachers of morality have indulged in reveries about the inner misery of evil men! How they have even lied to us about the misfortunes of passionate people! – yes, lied is the correct word here: they knew quite well about the exceeding good fortune of this sort of people, remaining deadly silent about it because it was a refutation of their theory, according to which all good fortune first arises with the destruction of passion and the silencing of the will. And as to what ultimately concerns the prescription of all these physicians of the soul and their extoling of a severe, radical cure, one is allowed to ask: is this life of ours really sufficiently painful and burdensome so as to exchange a stoic manner of life and petrification in preference to it? We do not deem ourselves *wretched enough* to find ourselves wretched in the stoic manner![60]

To conclude these historical considerations, then, Nietzsche did indeed find only "traces" of his doctrine in the writings of his precursors. What was missing was the spirit from which, and the history out of which, these reflections arose. Perhaps it is best to recall the context in which Nietzsche extoled his predecessors, which makes

---

Natur sei, und möchtet alles Dasein nur nach eurem eignen Bilde Dasein machen – als eine ungeheure ewige Verherrlichung und Verallgemeinerung des Stoizismus! Mit aller eurer Liebe zur Wahrheit zwingt ihr euch so lange, so beharrlich, so hypnotisch-starr, die Natur *falsch,* nämlich stoisch zu sehn . . ."

[60] *Ibid., Die Fröhliche Wissenschaft,* p. 189: "Was haben die **Moralprediger** vom inneren 'Elend' der bösen Menschen phantasiert! Was haben sie gar vom Unglücke der leidenschaftlichen Menschen uns *vorgelogen*! ja, lügen ist hier das rechte Wort: sie haben um das überreiche Glück dieser Art von Menschen recht wohl gewusst, aber es totgeschwiegen, weil es eine Wiederlegung ihrer Theorie war, nach der alles Glück erst mit der Vernichtung der Leidenschaft und dem Schweigen des Willens entsteht! Und was zuletzt das Rezept aller dieser Seelen-Ärzte betrifft und ihre Anpreisung einer harten radikalen Kur, so ist es erlaubt zu fragen: ist dieses unser Leben wirklich schmerzhaft und lästig genug, um mit Vorteil eine stoische Lebensweise und Versteinerung dagegen einzutauschen? Wir befinden uns *nicht schlecht genug,* um uns auf stoische Art schlecht befinden zu müssen!"

clear not only what he shared with them, but the sense in which his orientation was profoundly different. Nietzsche begins this aphorism with a reflection on the meaning of tragedy, as he had discussed it in his own book, *The Twilight of the Idols:*

"Saying Yes to life even in its strangest and hardest problems, the will to life rejoicing over its own inexhaustibility even in the very *sacrifice* of its highest types – that is what I call Dionysian, *that* is what I guessed to be the bridge to the psychology of the *tragic* poet. *Not* in order to be liberated from terror and pity, not in order to purge oneself of a dangerous affect by its vehement discharge – Aristotle misunderstood it that way – but in order to be *oneself* the eternal joy of becoming, beyond all terror and pity – that which included even joy in destroying . . ." In this sense I have the right to regard myself as the first *tragic philosopher* – that is, the most extreme antithesis and antipode of a pessimistic philosopher. Before me the transformation of the Dionysian into a philosophic pathos does not exist: *tragic wisdom* is lacking; I have sought in vain for signs of it even among the *great* Greek philosophers, those belonging to the two centuries *before* Socrates. I still retained a doubt about Heraclitus in whose company I feel better, more cheerful than anywhere else. Saying Yes to the flux *and destruction,* the decisive element in a Dionysian philosophy, saying Yes to contradiction and strife, *becoming,* together with the radical rejection of even the concept "*being*" – in this I must, in any case, acknowledge that which has the closest affinity to my thought hitherto. The doctrine of the "eternal recurrence," that is, of the unconditioned and infinitely repeated circularity of all things – this doctrine of Zarathustra's *could* in the final analysis already have been taught by Heraclitus. At a minimum, there are traces of it in the Stoics, who inherited almost all of their fundamental ideas from Heraclitus.[61]

---

[61] GOA *Nachlass* XV, *Ecce Homo,* 65: " 'Das Jasagen zum Leben selbst noch in seinen fremdesten und härtesten Problemen; der Wille zum Leben, im *Opfer* seiner höchsten Typen der eignen Unerschöpflichkeit frohwerdend – *das* nannte ich dionysisch, das verstand ich als Brücke zur Psychologie des *tragischen* Dichters. *Nicht* um von Schrecken und Mitleiden loszukommen, nicht um sich von einem gefährlichen Affekt durch eine vehemente Entladung zu reinigen – so missverstand es Aristoteles –: sondern um, über Schrecken und Mitleiden hinaus, die ewige Lust des Werdens selbst zu Sein – jene Lust, die auch noch die Lust am Vernichten in sich schliesst . . .' In diesem Sinne habe ich das Recht, mich selber als den ersten *tragischen Philosophen* zu verstehen – das heisst den äussersten Gegensatz und Antipoden eines pessimistischen Philosophen. Vor mir gibt es diese Umsetzung des dionysischen in ein philosophisches Pathos nicht: es fehlt die *tragische Weisheit* – ich habe vergebens nach Anzeichen davon selbst bei den *grossen* Griechen der Philosophie, die zwei Jahrhunderte *vor* Sokrates, gesucht. Ein Zweifel blieb mir zurück bei Heraklit, in dessen Nähe überhaupt mir wärmer, mir wohler zumute wird als irgendwo sonst. Die Bejahung des Vergehens *und Vernichtens,* das Entscheidende in einer dionysischen Philosophie, das Jasagen zu Gegensatz und Krieg, das Werden, mit radi-

If traditional metaphysics (including the Stoic ethic) had assumed plenary and defective modes of being, Nietzsche's "tragic wisdom" affirms each moment of cosmic change as sacred. If traditional metaphysics had sought release from the temporal, the senses, pain, passion, deception, from becoming, Nietzsche affirms each as an indispensable moment of self-realization: "Have you ever said Yes to a single joy? Oh my friends, then you said Yes too to all woe. All things are entangled . . . if ever you wanted once, twice . . . then you wanted *all* back . . ."[62] All joy wants the eternity of *all* things." [63] This affirmation of becoming differs from the docile acceptance which had characterized nihilism, in that it is born of an intense reflection bequeathed by the twilight of past idols.

Since mankind had fallen heir to the doctrine of becoming after the destruction of the "true world" but had failed to meditate or experience its meaning, they had inherited a becoming not yet shorn of goals. While affirming the temporal structure of all entities, the positive sciences, technology, and Darwinism had nonetheless retained elements of the abolished "true world." This brand of nihilism, the inverted other-worldliness, also possessed its "beyond": the future. The myth of progress, the last enduring secular-collective goal, is the culmination of nihilism, for Nietzsche, in so far as it eliminates the intense burden of self-overcoming, by submerging man in a mechanical and collective future redemption. Nietzsche's "tragic" affirmation of becoming, therefore, has a dual aspect. On the one hand, it must be affirmed without the imposition of goals. There is no given purpose exterior, anterior, or superior to the eternal circularity of all things: "The eternal recurrence of all things excludes every goal and purpose: Let us beware of inserting a goal, a striving, in this circularity . . ."[64]

kaler Ablehnung auch selbst des Begriffs *'Sein'* – darin muss ich unter allen Umständen das mir Verwandteste anerkennen, was bisher gedacht worden ist. Die Lehre von der 'ewigen Wiederkunft,' das heisst vom unbedingten und unendlich wiederholten Kreislauf aller Dinge – diese Lehre Zarathustras könnte zuletzt auch schon von Heraklit gelehrt worden sein. Zum mindestens hat die Stoa, die fast alle ihre grundsätzlichen Vorstellungen von Heraklit geerbt hat, Spuren davon."

[62] GOA VI, *Also Sprach Zarathustra,* 469: "Sagtet ihr jemals Ja zu einer Lust? Oh, meine Freunde, so sagtet ihr Ja auch zu allem Wehe. Alle Dinge sind Verkettet . . . wolltet ihr jemals Ein Mal zweimal . . . so wolltet ihr *alles* zurück."

[63] *Ibid.,* 470: "Alle Lust will *aller* Dinge Ewigkeit."

[64] GOA *Nachlass,* XII, 60: "Die ewige Wiederkunft aller Dinge entbehrt jedes Zieles und Zweckes: Hüten wir uns, diesem Kreislauf ein Streben, ein Ziel beizulegen."

We have invented the concept 'goal': in reality there is no goal." [65] Without goals and with the absence of a higher and a lower as *given* realities, becoming *is* being: "That everything returns is the most extreme approximation of a world of becoming to that of being." [66] On the other hand, the abolition of extrinsic goals does not imply a total and unconditioned relativity. In place of a fixed categorical imperative, Nietzsche's eternal recurrence asserts what I shall call an existential imperative: "My doctrine declares: the task is to live in such a way that you must wish to live again . . ." [67] While rejecting rigid normative criteria in ethics, Nietzsche affirms an ethical-psychological dimension. That which possesses value is that which can be willed unto eternity. With the loss of an absolute instrument for the judgment of conduct, the "that" which can be willed is no longer a single act, but a mode of being; a life. Whether or not a life is worthy of infinite repetition becomes Nietzsche's principle of selection and redemption.

Those who have argued that the doctrine of eternal recurrence is a disguised ethical imperative [68] were only partially correct. The doctrine of eternal recurrence may function as a regulative principle, but surely not a Kantian imperative. For, the positive value of Kant's deontological ethic is to be found in the criterion of universalizability when applied to *specific* acts, without regard to their consequences. Whereas the maxim (principle) governing a specific act will stand or founder on the rock of universalizability, in Kant, Nietzsche's eternal recurrence contains no normative criteria when applied to acts, beyond the subjective judgment that deems them *infinitely* worthwhile. But there is an even more serious defect in the argument that the eternal recurrence notion is analogous to Kant's categorical imperative. Kant's search for *a priori* synthetic principles in ethics of necessity postulated man's freedom. It was precisely because man is not only a phenomenal being but a noumenal being as well, that the *a priori* synthetic judgments of theoretical reason were inadequate in-

---

[65] GOA *Nachlass,* XIII, 101: "Wir haben den Begriff Ziel erfunden: in der Realität fehlt der Zweck."

[66] GOA *Nachlass,* XVI, 101: "Das alles wiederkehrt, ist die extremste Annäherung einer Welt des Werdens an die des Seins."

[67] GOA *Nachlass,* XII, 64: "Meine Lehre sagt: so leben, dass du wünschen musst, wieder zu leben, ist die Aufgabe . . ."

[68] Löwith, Simmel, Vaihinger, Oehler; in fact, the vast majority of Nietzsche critics.

struments for valid thinking about the conduct of life. Yet Nietzsche's doctrine of eternal recurrence, unlike Kant's ethics, seems to imply a strict determinism. If all things recur eternally in an identical pattern, backward and forward, then no act of volition can initiate a new cycle. If my future, as yet unknown to me, is governed by an inviolable decree merely repeating a life I have already lived innumerable times, then the immediate experience of my own freedom is, at bottom, an illusion. If the shock of eternal recurrence is to liberate our creative powers, then the insistence upon the eternal recurrence *of the same* announces the vanity and futility of all striving. And yet, Nietzsche's doctrine hovers within this tension: "I will return, – not to a new life or a better life or a similar life: – I shall eternally return to this same and identical life . . ."[69]

This strict determinism distinguishes Nietzsche not only from Kant, but from the Stoics and Spinoza as well. For Spinoza's deterministic claims do not involve the repetition of previous existences; hence they allow man the dignity of recognizing his continuity within Nature and liberate him from human bondage precisely through this awareness. Although there are no cleavages in Nature, hence man's role is not a "free" creation, man's fate is not foretold in Spinoza.

If our destiny is predetermined in the doctrine of eternal recurrence, how can this awareness shatter or transform us? Nietzsche seems to imply that our awareness of the fate of our existence, as an individual and cosmic repetition, calls for an even more radical affirmation. This may not be at all absurd upon reflection.

The eternal recurrence, the most radical of all determinisms, might be an effective notion because it nowhere implies a memory of previous states.

This moment has occurred an infinity of times before, as has its consequences and outcome. Yet, individual memory only functions within each recurrence. Memory functions as a durational element within a recurrence. It does not transcend a specific cycle. It is not transphenomenal. And yet, according to the eternal recurrence notion, this moment is but a repetition of an infinity of identical moments. Consequently, whatever my life entails, I only know that it will recur eternally and, also, that the outcome of my action has been de-

---

[69] GOA VI, *Also Sprach Zarathustra*, 322: "Ich komme wieder, – nicht zu einen neuem Leben oder besseren Leben oder ähnlichen Leben: ich komme ewig wieder zu diesem gleichen und selbigen Leben."

creed unto all eternity. My conduct, although apparently free, has been fore-ordained.

Nietzsche consciously opposes himself to Plato in most of his writings. His distinctions between "true" and "apparent," being and becoming, carry with them the overtones of the Platonic dialectic. And just as Nietzsche sought to transvaluate Platonic values in aesthetics, so he attacks the theory of recollection through the doctrine of eternal recurrence. There is, for Nietzsche, no inherent region of Forms (*eidos, idea*) which the soul recalls. On the contrary, the mind cannot even recall its own ineluctable fate, while the world recurs in eternal and monotonous self-identity. I only know what my life has been unto all eternity *after* I come to know what it is and will be. There are no fortunes to be told.

The eternal recurrence poses an existential paradox. In the absence of a memory of previous states I am free to choose my own destiny. I do not know what I shall become except in so far as I actually choose. Still, the eternal recurrence intensifies the dynamics of choice, because whatever I choose to be that I shall be for infinite recurrences. There is no immortal soul, for each moment is immortal. Once a moment has passed it does not sink into a past forever beyond recall. It shall eternally recur.

This strange and puzzling doctrine enjoins us to become what we are (a phrase of which Nietzsche rarely tires) not merely in the sense that we must fulfill our inner nature. It admonishes us to stamp the character of eternity upon our lives. It is the most extreme intensification and revaluation of the moment, by eternalizing it. The eternal future is cast by our conduct in this life. Thus, through the interpenetration of an infinite future and infinite past within the finite present, the moment too is eternalized. Paradoxically, I am free to create my determined fate. But the eternal recurrence proclaims a fate which we can embrace, because it is one which we alone shape. The eternalization of the moment through eternal recurrence is the most extreme approximation of a world of becoming to that of being. That, after all, was Nietzsche's highest and most hoped for achievement.

The goal of life is not given but created-fated unto all eternity. If "the task is to live in such a way that you must wish to live again . . .," there is but a theoretical contradiction introduced by adding "you will *anyway"* [70] to this formulation. Existentially, by transforming the finite moment into a fated eternity (without a doctrine of "recollection"), Nietzsche calls for the sisyphian assumption of one's destiny; *amor fati:* "Before fate strikes us it should be guided ... once it has struck us, however, one should seek to love it ..." [71] The Necessary does not injure me; amor fati is my inner nature ..." [72] Yes! I only want to love that which is necessary! Yes! amor fati may be my last love!" [73] The transformation of the finite into the infinite, the moment into an eternity, freedom into necessity, and horror into love, is the "highest state which a philosopher can attain: to stand in a dionysian relation to existence – my formula for it is amor fati." [74]

Nietzsche sought to overcome the traditional flight from becoming, i.e., metaphysics, Christianity, and nihilism, with a single formulation. By transforming becoming *into* being all bifurcations of apparent and real, temporal and timeless, contingent and necessary, are abolished. At the same time, the aimlessness of becoming is transcended by transforming the moment into a fated eternity.

Man's redemption, then, resides in no "beyond," nor in a partial and glib affirmation of a fleeting world. The circularity of all that exists is redeemed in the total and unconditioned love of becoming, which is my creation and my fate.

"The doctrine of eternal recurrence as a hammer in the hand of the most powerful ..." [75] poses the question: "Do you want this once more and innumerable times more ..." [76] as "a doctrine strong enough to have the effect of breeding: strengthening the strong, paralyzing and breaking the worldweary." [77]

---

[70] GOA *Nachlass,* XII, 64: "Meine Lehre sagt: so leben, dass du wünschen musst, wieder zu leben, ist die Aufgabe – du wirst es *jedenfalls!"*

[71] *Ibid.,* 323: "Bevor das Schicksal uns trifft, soll man es führen ... hat es uns aber getroffen, so soll man es zu lieben suchen."

[72] **GOA VIII,** *Die Götzendämmerung,* 115: "Das Notwendige verletzt mich nicht; amor fati ist meine innerste Natur."

[73] GOA *Nachlass,* XII, 141: "Ja! Ich will nur das noch lieben, was notwendig ist! Ja! amor fati sei meine letzte Liebe!"

[74] GOA *Nachlass,* XVI, 383: "Höchster Zustand, den ein Philosoph erreichen kann: dionysisch zum Dasein stehen –: meine Formel dafür ist amor fati."

[75] GOA *Nachlass,* XVI, 321: "Die Lehre der ewigen Wiederkehr als Hammer in der Hand der Mächtigsten Menschen."

[76] GOA, VI, *Die Fröhliche Wissenschaft,* 291: "willst du dies noch ein Mal und noch unzählige Male?"

[77] GOA *Nachlass,* XVI, 279: "Eine Lehre, stark genug, um züchten zu werken: stärkend für die Starken, lähmend und zerbrechend für die Weltmüden."

The doctrine of eternal recurrence is, in its central intention, necessarily an axiology and cosmology. Each is a necessary condition without which the doctrine cannot "overcome" the devaluation of the "apparent" world, allegedly affected by Platonic-Christian metaphysics, and consummated in post-Enlightenment "nihilism." But the existential imperative which the doctrine of eternal recurrence asserts is responsive to an aesthetic vision, indeed a "tragic" vision of reality, rather than an ethical one. The imperative is informed by an aesthetic metaphysics which conceives man as part and parcel of a fated natural order, in which this natural order is, paradoxically, constantly created by man's struggle with his own life. There are no values, ethical values, which are to be deduced from the recurring cycle of being. What is required, so Nietzsche believes, is a sisyphian affirmation of existence, a Dionysian Yea-saying, in the face of fate. Viewed from the context of Nietzsche's own development, this doctrine of eternal recurrence brings to fruition the task he had begun in his earliest work, *The Birth of Tragedy:* "This whole artist metaphysics might be called arbitrary, superfluous, fantastic . . . Yet, in its essential traits, it already reveals that spirit which will later defy and resist courageously any moral interpretation and meaning of existence . . . here we find, perhaps for the first time, a pessimism 'beyond good and evil'." [78]

[78] Karl Schlechta (ed.) *Werke in Drei Bänden* (Carl Hanser Verlag: München, 1955), vol. I, p. 15: "Diese Ganze Artisten-Metaphysik mag man willkürlich, müssing, phantastisch nennen . . . das Wesentliche daran ist, dass sie bereits einen Geist verräth, der sich einmal auf jede Gefahr hin die moralische Ausdeutung und Bedeutsamkeit des Daseins zur Wehre setzen wird . . . hier kündigt sich, vielleicht zum ersten Male, ein Pessimismus 'jenseits von Gut und Böse' an."

PART II

HEIDEGGER'S METAHISTORY OF PHILOSOPHY

CHAPTER I

HEIDEGGER AND THE TRADITION

It has been observed[1] that few philosophers have devoted as much of their energy to an analysis of the writings of others as has Martin Heidegger. His reflections on the achievements of his predecessors forms an organic part of his own philosophy. Among these predecessors he has devoted more attention to Nietzsche than to any other thinker.[2] This has not always been the case.

In *Being and Time*[3] Nietzsche is hardly mentioned. He is referred to only three times[4] in passing, and not at all in relation to the central task of the book – asking the question of the meaning of Being anew. Heidegger's projected plans for a book entitled *Time and Being*,[5] of which *Being and Time* was to have been the first part, also ignore Nietzsche. This is significant. The projected book was to consist of a recapitulation and destruction of the history of ontology.[6] It was in this work that Heidegger had intended to show how the Being question had been fatefully misunderstood from Aristotle to Kant: "The destruction of the history of ontology is essentially bound up with the way the question of Being is formulated, and it is possible only within such a formulation. In the framework of our treatise, which aims at working that question out in principle, we can carry out this destruction only with regard to stages of that history which are in principle decisive."[7] It would appear, by omission, that Nietzsche's philosophy

---

[1] Karl Löwith, *Heidegger: Denker in Dürftiger Zeit* (Frankfurt: S. Fisher, 1953).

[2] *Nietzsche*, vol. I, II (Pfullingen, 1961); *Vorträge und Aufsätze* (Pfullingen, 1954); *Holzwege* (Frankfurt am Main, 1950).

[3] *Sein und Zeit* (7. Aufl., Tübingen, 1953).

[4] *Ibid.*, pp. 264, 272n vi, 396.

[5] Cf. *Ibid.*, introduction.

[6] *Ibid.*, pp. 19–27.

[7] *Ibid.*, p. 23: "Im Rahmen der vorliegenden Abhandlung, die eine grundsätzliche Ausarbeitung der Seinsfrage zum Ziel hat, kann die zur Fragestellung

was not regarded as a "decisive" stage in the history of ontology, as Heidegger understood the question of Being in 1927. Yet, this thinker became increasingly important for the later Heidegger. Not long after the publication of *Being and Time,* and for the following decades, Heidegger treats Nietzsche as an equal among the giants of Western thought.

In the projected part II of *Being and Time,* the "phenomenological destruction of the history of ontology"[8] was to have been accomplished in three phases; a consideration of "Kant's doctrine of the schematism and time . . ., the ontological foundation of Descartes' 'cogito sum'"[9] in its relation to medieval ontology, and an analysis of "Aristotle's essay on time as providing a way of discriminating the phenomenal basis and limits of ancient ontology."[10]

The reasons which help to explain Heidegger's failure to systematically complete this project to-date need not concern us here. However, on the basis of his later works, it is clear that Heidegger's view of Western ontology had changed in emphasis after his earliest publication. After *Being and Time* the tradition's forgetfulness of Being is no longer viewed as beginning with Aristotle and ending with Kant as "decisive" phases. The matrix of *Seinsvergenssenheit,* the forgetfulness of Being, shifts from Aristotle and Kant to Plato and Nietzsche, as the *terminus a quo* and *terminus ad quem.*

Heidegger himself suggests this shift in emphasis in his preface to a two volume Nietzsche study, albeit elliptically. "The publication, when reflected upon as a whole, ought to offer an insight into the path of thought which I have travelled from 1930 to the *Letter on Humanism* (1947). For the two small lectures, *Plato's Theory of Truth* (1942) and *On the Essence of Truth* (1943), which were published during the aforesaid period, were already conceived during the years 1930–31."[11] This brief prefatory remark sheds some light on the nature of

wesenhaft gehörende und lediglich innerhalb ihrer mögliche Destruktion der Geschichte der Ontologie nur an grundsätzlich entscheidenden Stationen dieser Geschichte durchgeführt werden."

[8] *Ibid.,* p. 39: ". . . phänomenologischen Destruktion der Geschichte der Ontologie . . ."

[9] *Ibid.,* p. 49: "Kants Lehre vom Schematismus und der Zeit . . . Das ontologische Fundament des 'cogito sum Descartes.'"

[10] *Ibid.:* "Die Abhandlung des Aristoteles über die Zeit als Diskrimen der phänomenalen Basis und der Grenzen der antiken Ontologie."

[11] *Nietzsche,* vol. I (Pfullingen, 1961), p. 10: "Die Veröffentlichung möchte, als Ganzes nachgedacht, zugleich einen Blick auf den Denkweg verschaffen, den

Heidegger's thought path from 1930–47. It suggests, first, that a continuity of thought exists during this period which centers on the phenomenon of truth, and, second, that Heidegger's conception of the nature of truth is intimately connected with the philosophy of Plato and Nietzsche. Plato's transformation of *alétheia,* and Nietzsche's ultimate expression of truth as subjectivity in the will to power, constitute central and recurrent themes in Heidegger's understanding of Being and metaphysics, as will be exhibited below. To be sure, Heidegger also intended the above quotation to shed light on the *Kehre,* the reversal from Dasein to Being, in his thought. Heidegger intended to show that the controversial reversal in his thinking was not a product of reflections arrived at in 1947, with the publication of the *Letter on Humanism,* but the expression of thoughts implicitly developing from 1930 on.

In the light of the above remarks, it should be clear that Heidegger's conception of Nietzsche's doctrine of eternal recurrence, as the last metaphysical thought of the West, becomes intelligible only after we know what Heidegger came to understand as "metaphysics" in the period after 1930. On the basis of his own testimony, Heidegger's understanding of metaphysics is intimately connected with his understanding of the nature of truth.

Metaphysics is not only a traditional branch of philosophy for Heidegger. He frequently uses the term in a broad sense in which it is said to express man's relationship to the Being of beings. In this sense Heidegger regards man's relationship to what is as metaphysical.

In so far as man relates to beings, he represents being to himself with reference to the fact that it is, what and how it is, how it might be and ought to be; in short, he represents being with reference to its Being. This re-presentation is thinking . . . In whatever manner man may re-present beings as such to himself he represents them in view if their Being. Because of this man always goes beyond beings and crosses over to Being. In Greek, "beyond" is *meta.* Hence man's every relationship to beings as such is metaphysical.[12]

ich seit 1930 bis zum 'Brief über den Humanismus' (1947), gegangen bin. Denn die zwei kleinen, während der genannten Zeit gedruckten Vorträge 'Platons Lehre von der Wahrheit' (1942), und 'Vom Wesen der Wahrheit' (1943) sind bereits in den Jahren 1930/31 enstanden."
[12] *Vorträge und Aufsätze* (Pfullingen, 1954), p. 112: "Insofern der Mensch sich zum Seienden verhält, stellt er das Seiende hinsichtlich dessen vor, dass es ist, was es und wie es ist, wie es sein möchte und sein soll, kurz gesagt: das

Quotations such as these could be multiplied a hundred-fold. Heidegger conceives metaphysics as the mode of Western man's relationship to Being. Man is the *animal metaphysicum* in this account. This is the broader sense of metaphysics, as Heidegger uses that term, in the light of which even his own pursuit of Being is but a continuation of a long tradition. However, Heidegger uses the term "metaphysics" in a much narrower sense as well. It is of some importance to distinguish the two senses.

The narrower sense of "metaphysics," for Heidegger, constitutes a certain way in which Being has been understood since Plato. In that context the term is generally synonymous with the history of Western philosophy. It is this narrower sense of "metaphysics" which Heidegger sought to overcome, precisely in the name of a fundamental ontology which finds its roots in an older "metaphysics" – that of the pre-Socratic philosophers. In effect, Heidegger's endeavor to reawaken the allegedly lost sense of Being is an attempt to recall traditional metaphysics from its obliviousness to its own nature – the pursuit of Being.

Although to my knowledge Heidegger nowhere makes an attempt explicitly to disengage these two very distinct meanings he attaches to the word "metaphysics," without recognizing this distinction his attempted "destruction" of the history of metaphysics could be easily misunderstood. Since "man always goes beyond beings and crosses over to Being,"[13] and is necessarily a metaphysical being, Heidegger's objections to "metaphysics" should not be construed as an objection to the nature of man. His objections to metaphysics are always directed to the *way* in which Being has been understood within what we call "classical" philosophy from Plato to Nietzsche. Hence the metaphysical being, man, has historically understood his world within the context of a metaphysics which is allegedly inadequate to the comprehension of Being which Heidegger proposes.

Heidegger's earliest interest in philosophy was stirred by Franz

---

Seiende hinsichtlich seines Seins. Dieses Vor-stellen ist das Denken ... Wie immer auch der Mensch das Seiende als solches vorstellen mag, er stellt es im Hinblick auf dessen Sein vor. Durch diesen Hinblick geht er über das Seiende immer schon hinaus und hinüber zum Sein. Hinüber heisst griechisch *meta*. Darum ist jedes Verhältnis des Menschen zum Seienden als solches in sich metaphysisch."

[13] *Ibid.:* "Geht er über das Seiende immer schon hinaus und hinüber zum Sein."

Brentano's doctoral dissertation, *On the Manifold Sense of Being in Aristotle,*[14] which he studied in 1907. As Heidegger clearly states in his preface to a book by William Richardson, Brentano's dissertation suggested the questions which were to occupy all of his later thought:

what is the pervasive, simple, unified determination of Being that permeates all of its multiple meanings? This question awakens the following questions: what, then, does Being mean? In what manner (why and how) does the Being of beings unfold in the four modes which Aristotle constantly affirms, but whose common origin he leaves undetermined? It suffices to note the names assigned to them in the language of the philosophical tradition in order to be struck by the fact that they appear, at first, irreconcilable. Being as attribute, Being as potentiality and actuality, Being as truth, Being as schema of the categories. What meaning of Being is expressed in these four headings? How can they be brought into comprehensible accord?

This accord can only be grasped after first raising and elucidating the question: whence does Being as such (not only beings as beings) receive its determination?[15]

The single underlying question, What is the meaning of Being?, first received explicit attention in *Being and Time.* In it Heidegger concluded that Being has meant three fundamental things in the philosophical tradition: "the most universal concept,"[16] "the undefinable"[17] and the "self-evident."[18]

As the most universal of all concepts, Being is included within any conception whatsoever. All objects of thought imply Being, in the sense that nothing is not an object of consciousness. "Real" and "un-

[14] *Von der mannigfachen Bedeutung des Seienden nach Aristoteles* (Freiburg im Bresgau, 1862).

[15] William Richardson, *Heidegger; Through Phenomenology to Thought* (The Hague, 1963), p. XI: "Welches ist die alle mannigfachen Bedeutungen durchherrschende einfache, einheitliche Bestimmung von Sein? Inwiefern (weshalb und wie) entfaltet sich das Sein des Seienden in die von Aristoteles stets nur festgestellten in ihrer gemeinsamen Herkunft unbestimmt gelassenen vier Weisen? Es genügt, diese in der Sprache der philosophischen Überlieferung auch nur zu nennen, um von dem zunächst unvereinbar Erscheinenden betroffen zu werden: Sein als Eigenschaft, Sein als Möglichkeit und Wirklichkeit, Sein als Wahrheit, Sein als Schema der Kategorien. Welcher Sinn von Sein spricht in diesen vier Titeln? Wie lassen sie sich in einen verstehbaren Einklang bringen?

"Diesen Einklang können wir erst dann vernehmen, wenn zuvor gefragt und geklärt wird: Woher empfängt das Sein als solches (nicht nur das Seiende als Seiendes) seine Bestimmung?"

[16] *Sein und Zeit* (7. Aufl., Tübingen, 1953), p. 3.

[17] *Ibid.,* p. 4.

[18] *Ibid.*

real," "perceived" and "imagined" entities all "are." It is their mode
of being which is, derivatively, distinguished. The mode of being appropriate to a unicorn, for example, involves its status as an imaginary object. A unicorn does not exist in the extensional sense i.e., it
lacks spatio-temporal location. The "unreal" does "not exist" in the
sense in which, conventionally, it is said to lack a spatiotemporal
referent. As an object of the imagination, however, the unicorn "exists" and possesses the mode of being ascribed to imaginary objects.
This perhaps unHeideggerian way of stating the matter does not suggest that "Being," "real object" and "imaginary object" are the same
in any sense. No object nor object of thought is Being (Sein). Rather,
it is *a* being (Seiendes). Hence, in traditional metaphysics,

> The universality of "being" does not define that realm of beings which
> is uppermost when this is articulated conceptually according to genus and
> species: *auto to on logos*. The "universality" of Being *"transcends"* any
> universality of genus ... So if it is said that "Being" is the most universal
> concept, this cannot mean that it is one which is clearest and in no further
> need of discussion. The concept of "Being" is, rather, the most obscure.[19]

Heidegger distinguishes two spheres, the ontic and the ontological.
The former refers to all beings ("real," "unreal," "imagined," "delusory"), the latter to the Being (*Sein*) of beings. Being transcends any
genus, historically understood, because it lacks the generic determinations which discriminate and differentiate the ontic sphere. It is for
this reason that Being has been conceived by the tradition as the most
universal concept. Being is the most universal of all concepts and is
presupposed by every inquiry. "Ontological inquiry is indeed more
primordial ,as over against the ontical inquiry of the positive sciences.
But it remains itself naive and opaque if in its researches into the
Being of beings it fails to discuss the meaning of Being in general."[20]

---

[19] *Ibid.*, p. 3: "Aber die 'Allgemeinheit' von 'Sein' ist nicht die der *Gattung*.
'Sein' umgrenzt nicht die oberste Region des Seienden, sofern dieses nach Gattung und Art begrifflich artikuliert ist: *auto to on logos*. Die 'allgemeinheit' des
Seins *'übersteigt'* alle gattungsmässige Allgemeinheit ... Wenn man demnach
sagt: 'Sein' ist der allgemeinste Begriff, so kann das nicht heissen, er ist der
klarste und aller weiteren Eröterung unbedürftig. Der Begriff des 'Seins' ist vielmehr der dunkelste."
[20] *Ibid.*, p. 11: "Ontologisches Fragen ist zwar gegenüber dem ontischen
Fragen der positiven Wissenschaften ursprünglicher. Es bleibt aber selbst naiv
und undurchsichtig, wenn es seine Nachforschungen nach dem Sein des Seienden
den Sinn von Sein überhaupt unerötert lassen."

That Being has been conceived as undefinable follows from its universality and generality.

In any attempted definition of the form "Being is X," it is the copula, not only the subject, which is the object of the definition. The procedure is doomed to circularity because the copula constitutes a part of the definiendum. This is a consequence of the fact that while every instance of Being, every being, may have specific determinations, these determinations define it as *a* being, not Being. The range of application of the term "Being" is inexhaustible, since everything that exists belongs to the class "Being." The extension of Being governs the totality of that-which-is and its intension is indeterminable.

"Being" cannot, in fact, be conceived as a being; *enti non additur aliqua natura:* nor can "Being" acquire such a character as to have the term "being" applied to it. "Being" cannot be derived from higher concepts by definition, nor can it be presented through lower ones. But does it follow from this that "Being" no longer offers a problem? Not at all; we can infer only that "Being" cannot be something like beings. Thus we cannot apply to Being the sort of determination – the "definition" of traditional logic, which itself has its foundations in ancient ontology – which provides, within certain limits, a justifiable way of defining being. The undefinability of Being does not dispose of the question of its meaning, rather, it directly demands it.[21]

That Being is self-evident is the third sense in which it has been traditionally understood, according to Heidegger. Thus, to use Heidegger's own examples, everyone understands that Being is assumed to be self-evident in the assertions "The sky *is* blue" or "I *am* happy."[22] Neither proposition overtly interrogates Being. Yet, these utterances are possible because beings are and, as was said above, beings *are* because Being is. It should be noted, in passing, that Heidegger does not mean by "self-evident" any strict logical criterion. Being is not self-evident in the logical sense that its denial involves a self-

[21] *Ibid.*, p. 4: " 'Sein' kann in der tat nicht als Seiendes begriffen werden; enti non additur aliqua natura: 'Sein' kann nicht so zur Bestimmtheit kommen, dass ihm Seiendes Zugesprochen wird. Das Sein ist definitorisch aus höheren Begriffen nicht abzuleiten und durch niedere nicht darzustellen. Aber folgt hieraus, dass 'Sein' kein Problem mehr bieten kann? Mitnichten; gefolgert kann nur werden: 'Sein' ist nicht so etwas wie Seiendes. Daher ist die in gewissen Grenzen berechtigte Bestimmungsart von Seiendem – die 'Definition' der traditionellen Logik, die selbst ihre Fundamente in der antiken Ontologie hat – auf das Sein nicht anwendbar. De Undefinierbarkeit des Seins dispensiert nicht von der Frage nach seinem Sinn, sondern fordert dazu gerade auf."

[22] *Ibid.*, p. 4.

contradiction. It is equally obvious that the truth of the proposition "there is such a thing as Being" could be denied without entailing the falsehood of the propositions "The sky is blue" or "I am happy." By the "self-evidence" of Being, Heidegger means that the tradition has generally acknowledge our pre-discursive awareness of it. If propositions are about some-thing, the thing "is." And, again, it is the *is* (Being) which Heidegger is endeavoring to understand:

> "Being" is the self-evident concept. In all cognition, assertion, in every relationship to beings, in every relationship of oneself, some use is made of "Being" and the expression is intelligible "without further ado." Everyone understands: "They sky *is* blue"; "I *am* happy," and the like. But this average intelligibility merely demonstrates the unintelligibility. It makes manifest that in each relationship and Being towards beings as beings there lies an *a priori* enigma. The fact that we already live in an understanding of Being and that the meaning of Being is still veiled in darkness, demonstrates the fundamental necessity of repeating the question of "Being" again.[23]

Heidegger states, even more explicitly, that we are aware of Being, pre-analytically, and that any ontology must take this into account:

> Inquiry, as a kind of seeking, must be guided beforehand by what is sought. So the meaning of Being must already be available to us in some way. As we have intimated, we always conduct our activities within an understanding of Being. Out of this understanding there arises both the explicit question of the meaning of Being and the tendency that leads us toward its conception. We do not *know* what "Being" means. But even if we ask "What is 'Being'?", we remain within an understanding of the "is," although we are unable to fix conceptually what that "is" signifies. We do not even know the horizon in terms of which that meaning is to be grasped and fixed. *But this vague average understanding of Being is still a fact.*[24]

---

[23] *Ibid.,* p. 4: "Das 'Sein' ist der selbstverständliche Begriff. In allem Erkennen, Aussagen, in jedem Verhalten zu Seiendem, in jedem Sich-zu-sich-selbstverhalten wird von 'Sein' gebrauch gemacht, und der Ausdruck ist dabei 'ohne weiteres' verständlich. Jeder versteht: 'Der Himmel *ist* blau'; 'ich *bin* froh' und dgl. Allein diese durchschnittliche Verständlichkeit demonstriert nur die Unverständlichkeit. Sie macht offenbar, dass in jedem Verhalten und Sein zu Seiendem als Seiendem *a priori* ein Rätsel liegt. Dass wir je schon in einem Seinsverständnis leben und der Sinn von Sein zugleich in Dunkel gehüllt ist, beweist die grundsätzliche Notwendigkeit, die Frage nach dem Sinn von 'Sein' zu wiederholen."

[24] *Ibid.,* p. 5: "Als Suchen bedarf des Fragen einer vorgängigen Leitung vom Gesuchten her. Der Sinn von Sein muss uns daher schon in gewisser Weise verfügbar sein. Angedeutet wurde: wir bewegen uns immer schon in einem Seins–verständnis. Aus ihm heraus erwächst die Ausdrückliche Frage nach dem Sinn von Sein und die Tendenz zu dessen Begriff. Wir *wissen* nicht, was 'Sein' besagt.

Heidegger regarded the traditional criteria of universality, undefinability and self-evidence, as inadequate from the very beginning: "what is the pervasive, simple, unified determination of Being that permeates all of its multiple meanings?. . . How can they be brought into comprehensible accord?"[25] This conviction concerning the inadequacy of the traditional comprehension of Being led Heidegger into two directions simultaneously. First, he attempted to reveal the manner in which the meaning of Being had fallen into oblivion in traditional metaphysics (the recapitulated "destruction of the history of ontology"), in an endeavor, second, to re-awaken the primordial sense of Being which this tradition had allegedly dissimulated.

Heidegger has argued that the three criteria, universality, undefinability and self-evidence, are not merely inadequate but are *products* of an inadequate approach to Being; metaphysics. Rather than simply bearing the responsibility for the tradition's incapacity to grasp the primordial sense of Being, the three criteria become the *consequence* of a metaphysical endeavor to understand Being. For Heidegger, the criteria are, at bottom, derived from philosophy's success in applying the categorial mode of thought to beings, to entities. Universality, undefinability and self-evidence, may be appropriate ways of addressing ourselves to beings, to the ontic, but are inappropriate for the attempt to understand the meaning of Being. Heidegger is persuaded that the application of these criteria to Being has resulted in treating it as *a* being. In essence, the criteria are conceptual categories which, as categories, render Being obscure. Heidegger, on the other hand, is concerned with retrieving the pre-discursive, ontological sense of Being.

We have shown at the outset (# 1) not only that the question of the meaning of Being is one that has not been attended to and one which has been inadequately formulated, but that it has become quite forgotten despite all our interest in "metaphysics." Greek ontology and its history, which in their numerous filiations and distortions determine the conceptual character of philosophy even today, demonstrate that when Dasein understands either itself or Being in general, it does so in terms of the "world," and that the ontology which has thus arisen has deteriorated into

Aber schon wenn wir fragen: 'was *ist* 'Sein'?' halten wir uns in einem Verständnis des 'ist,' ohne dass wir begrifflich fixieren könnten, was das 'ist' bedeutet. Wir kennen nicht einmal den Horizont, aus dem her wir den Sinn fassen und fixieren sollten. *Dieses durchschnittliche und vage Seinsverständnis ist ein Faktum.*

[25] Cf. note number 14.

a tradition in which it gets reduced to something self-evident – merely material for reworking (as it was for *Hegel*). In the Middle Ages this uprooted Greek ontology became a fixed body of doctrine ... With the peculiar character which the *Scholastics* give it, Greek ontology has, in its essentials, travelled the path that leads through the *Disputationes Metaphysicae* of *Suarez* to the "metaphysics" and transcendental philosophy of modern times, determining even the foundations and the aims of *Hegel's* "logic." In the course of this history, certain distinctive domains of Being have come into view and have served as the primary guides for subsequent problematics (the *ego cogito* of *Descartes,* the subject, the "I," reason, spirit, person) but these all remain uninterrogated as to their Being and its structure, in accordance with the thoroughgoing way in which the question of Being has been neglected. It is rather that the categorial content of traditional ontology has been carried over to these beings with corresponding formalizations and purely negative restrictions, or else dialectic has been called in for the purpose of interpreting the substantiality of the subject ontologically ...[26]

Basically, all ontology, no matter how rich and firmly compacted a system of categories it has at its disposal, remains blind and perverted from its ownmost aim, if it has not first adequately clarified the meaning of Being, and conceived this clarification as its fundamental task.[27]

---

[26] *Sein und Zeit* (7. Aufl., Tübingen, 1953), pp. 21–23: "Eingangs (# 1) wurde gezeigt, dass die Frage nach dem Sinn des Seins nicht nur unerledigt, nicht nur nicht zureichend gestellt, sondern bei allem Interesse für 'Metaphysik' in Vergessenheit gekommen ist. Die griechische Ontologie und ihre Geschichte, die durch mannigfache Filiationen und Verbiegungen hindurch noch heute die Begrifflichkeit der Philosophie bestimmt, ist der Beweis dafür, dass das Dasein sich selbst und das Sein überhaupt aus der 'Welt' her versteht und dass die so erwachsene Ontologie der Tradition verfällt, die sie zur Selbstverständlichkeit und zum bloss neu zu bearbeitenden Material (so für *Hegel*) herabsinken lässt. Diese entwurzelte griechische Ontologie wird im Mittelalter zum festen Lehrbestand ... In der *scholastischen* Prägung geht die griechische Ontologie im wesentlichen auf dem Wege über die *Disputationes metaphysicae* des *Suarez* in die 'Metaphysik' und Transzendentalphilosophie der Neuzeit über und bestimmt noch die Fundamente und Ziele der 'Logik' Hegels. Soweit im vorlauf dieser Geschichte bestimmte ausgezeichnete Seinsberzirke in den Blick kommen und fortan primär die Problematik leiten (das ego cogito Descartes', Subjekt, Ich, Vernunft, Geist, Person), bleiben diese, entsprechend dem durchgängigen Versäumnis der Seinsfrage, unbefragt auf Sein und Struktur ihres Seins. Vielmehr wird der kategoriale Bestand der traditionellen Ontologie mit entsprechenden Formalisierungen und lediglich negative Einschränkungen auf dieses Seiende übertragen, oder aber es wird in der Absicht auf eine ontologische Interpretation der Substanzialität des Subjekts die Dialektik zu Hilfe gerufen."

[27] *Ibid.,* p. 11: "*Alle Ontologie, mag sie über ein noch so reiches und festverklemmertes Kategoriensystem verfügen, bleibt im Grunde blind und eine Verkehrung ihrer eigensten Absicht, wenn sie nicht zuvor den Sinn von Sein zureichend geklärt und diese Klärung als ihre Fundamentalaufgabe begriffen hat.*"

In *What is Metaphysics?*, Heidegger posed the ontological problem by referring to Descartes' analogy: "Thus the whole of philosophy is like a tree; the roots are metaphysics, the trunk is physics and the branches that issue from the trunk are all the other sciences."[28] With reference to this analogy Heidegger asks: "In what soil do the roots of the tree of philosophy have their hold? Out of what ground do the roots – and through them the whole tree – receive their nourishing juices and strength? What element, concealed in the ground and soil, enters and lives in the roots that support and nourish the tree? In what is metaphysics secured and animated? What is metaphysics, viewed from its ground?"[29] The "ground" of metaphysics refers, here, to the Being of beings. The attempt to retrieve the ground of metaphysics forced Heidegger to a reflection upon the pre-metaphysical experience of Being, and its dramatic transformation in Plato's metaphysics: "Since Plato, thinking about the Being of beings becomes – 'philosophy' . . . The 'philosophy' first begun with Plato hereafter possesses the characteristic of that which is later called 'metaphysics'. . . Even the word 'metaphysics' is already molded in Plato's presentation."[30] Heidegger's critique of the criteria in terms of which Being has been historically understood is grounded in a critique of metaphysics as such, which Heidegger identifies as the ineluctable movement of philosophic thought from Plato to Nietzsche.

Heidegger's analysis of Plato attempts to show that a transformation occurs in the nature of truth in Plato's philosophy, as a consequence of which Being is subordinated to the correct perception of beings. This subordination, Heidegger maintains, characterizes the history of Western philosophy as metaphysics.

[28] *Was ist Metaphysik?* (5. Aufl., Frankfurt, 1949), p. 7: "Ainsi toute la philosophie est comme un arbre, dont les racines sont la Metaphysique, le tronc est la Physique, et les tranches que sortent de ce tronc sont toutes les autres sciences . . ."

[29] *Ibid.*, p. 7: "In welchem Boden finden die Wurzeln des Baumes der Philosophie ihren Halt? Aus welchem Grunde empfangen die Wurzeln und durch sie der ganze Baum die nährenden Säfte und Kräfte? Welches Element durchwebt, in Grund und Boden verborgen, die tragenden und nährenden Wurzeln des Baumes? Worin ruht und regt sich die Metaphysik? Was ist die Metaphysik von ihrem Grund her gesehen?"

[30] *Platons Lehre von der Wahrheit* (A. Francke, Bern, 1947), p. 49: "Seit Platon wird das Denken über das Sein des Seienden – 'Philosophie' . . . Die erst mit Platon beginnende 'Philosophie' aber hat fortan den Charakter dessen, was später 'Metaphysik' heisst . . . Ja sogar das Wort 'Metaphysik' ist in Platons Darstellung schon vorgeprägt."

Platons Lehre von der Wahrheit[31] is an interpretation of Plato's *Republic*, 514A – 517A; an interpretation of the allegory of the cave. It is a reflection upon the relationship between education (*paideia*), truth (*alétheia*) and the good (*agathon*), with the transformation of *alétheia* as the principal concern.

The allegory of the cave is, for Heidegger, an illustration of the nature and process of *paideia*. At each level of ascent – within the cave to the light, and out of the cave to the sun – the individual experiences a painful blinding. Each stage requires an adjustment and transformation in vision. This transformation in vision expresses the turning of the soul from what is disclosed in one region to what is disclosed within another. This is *paideia,* according to Heidegger. The relationship of *paideia,* in this new sense, to *alétheia* is not apparent because, as Heidegger sees it, we have not only misunderstood the nature of education but, more importantly, have misconceived the nature of *alétheia* by conceiving it as "truth." If *paideia* is a transition from one abode to another, affected by the soul's receptivity to what is disclosed within each region, then *alétheia* is disclosure itself: "At first truth meant what was wrested from a concealment. Truth, then, is just such a perpetual wresting-away in this manner of uncovering."[32]

Unlike the case of the two distinct senses in which Heidegger employs the term "metaphysics," the two senses in which he employs the term "truth" are made very explicit. Truth, conceived as *alétheia,* is the plenary mode; truth conceived as a correspondence between an idea and the thing it represents is a derivative mode. Because Heidegger invariably assigns the correspondence concept of truth to "metaphysics," understood in the restricted sense in which it designates the history of Western philosophy, we have called it the "epistemological" concept of truth. "Ontological" truth, on the other hand, designates disclosure itself – specifically, Heidegger's attempted disclosure of Being.

Heidegger's earliest systematic analysis of the epistemological concept of truth, as well as rejection of it, occurs in *Being and Time.*

Three theses characterize the way in which the essence of truth has

---

[31] A. Francke, Bern, 1947.
[32] *Ibid.,* p. 32: "Wahrheit bedeutet anfänglich das einer Verborgenheit Abgerungene. Wahrheit ist also solche Entringung jeweils in der Weise der Entbergung."

been traditionally conceived and the way it is supposed to have been first defined: (1) that the "locus" of truth is assertion (judgment); (2) that the essence of truth lies in the "agreement" of the judgment with its object; (3) that Aristotle, the father of logic, not only assigned truth to the judgment as its primordial locus, but has set going the definition of "truth" as "agreement." [33]

In keeping with the original emphasis in *Being and Time,* Heidegger asserts the presence of this conception of truth in Aristotle, Aquinas and Kant, (rather than Plato and Nietzsche), before continuing with his explicit analysis of the "epistemological" concept of truth. In the course of his analysis several important points are raised. The problem underlying what we have called the "epistemological" concept of truth, Heidegger points out, is the nature of the agreement – *adequatio, correspondentia, convenientia* – between a judgment and its object: "Every agreement, and therefore 'truth' as well, is a relation. But not every relation is an agreement." [34] Heidegger goes on to raise and answer in the negative the question whether the "agreement" can be conceived as a relation of equality. But "If it is impossible for *intellectus* and *res* to be equal because they are not of the same species, are they then perhaps similar?" [35] With reference to similarity as a possible basis for the relation called "agreement," Heidegger points out that within the judgment itself we must distinguish between the psychical process and the ideal content of judgment. Any "similarity" relation of a judgment to its object (truth) must refer to the ideal content, rather than the psychical processes of judgment. But such a distinction merely raises an additional problem: *"How is the relation between ideal being and real being to be grasped ontologically?"* [36] To this question, Heidegger maintains, the philosophic tradition has no meaningful answer: "Is it accidental that no headway has been

[33] *Sein und Zeit* (7. Aufl., Tübingen, 1953), p. 214: "Drei Thesen charakterisieren die traditionelle Auffassung des Wesens der Wahrheit und die Meinung über ihre erstmalige Definition: 1. Der 'Ort' der Wahrheit ist die Aussage (das Urteil) 2. Das Wesen der Wahrheit liegt in der 'Übereinstimmung' des Urteils mit seinem Gegenstand 3. Aristoteles, der Vater der Logik, hat sowohl die Wahrheit dem Urteil als ihrem ursprünglichen Ort zugewiesen, er hat auch die Definition der Wahrheit als 'Übereinstimmung' in Gang gebracht."

[34] *Ibid.,* p. 215: "Jede Übereinstimmung und somit auch 'Wahrheit' ist eine Beziehung. Aber nicht jede Beziehung ist Übereinstimmung."

[35] *Ibid.,* p. 216: "Wenn Gleichheit auf Grund der fehlenden Gleichartigkeit beider unmöglich ist, sind beide (intellectus und res) dann vielleicht ähnlich?"

[36] *Ibid.: "Wie soll die Beziehung zwischen ideale Seiendem und real Vorhandenem ontologisch gefasst werden?"*

made with this problem in over two thousand years?"[37] In fact, Heidegger goes even further in the sentence which immediately follows the preceding one, by suggesting that this entire procedure – trying to discern the nature of the *adequatio* which characterizes a truth relationship between *rei et intellectus* – may be fruitless: "Does the perversion of the problem already lie in the approach, in the ontologically unclarified separation of Real and Ideal?"[38] It is of some importance to emphasize that Heidegger not only discussed and rejected the "epistemoligical" concept of truth, as early as *Being and Time* (1927), but that he regarded it the sustaining one to be found in Western ontology. And, of course he suggested an alternative as well. The alternative, which I have called "ontological" truth, remains in its essential features the basis for his later critique of Plato and the history of metaphysics.

Heidegger indicates that what "truth" means is not so much a correspondence as it is a disclosure. Taking the sentence "the picture on the wall is hanging askew" as a true proposition, Heidegger points out that a person who turns to the wall and perceives that the picture in fact is hanging askew, merely confirms the truth of the proposition. "And what does one's perceiving of it demonstrate?"[39] It does not demonstrate that a correspondence exists between a mental content, expressed in the assertion, and a physically "real" picture hanging askew on the wall. If it does this, it does so derivatively. For Heidegger, the perceiving demonstrates "Nothing other than *that* it *is* the being itself which was intended in the assertion."[40] The shift in emphasis (in the locus of truth) from agreement to disclosure, stresses the fact that true propositions are true in so far as they disclose, reveal, uncover, the being they announce. As Heidegger puts it,

This disclosedness is confirmed when that which is put forward in the assertion (namely the being itself) shows itself *as that very same thing.* *"Confirmation"* signifies *the being's showing itself in its selfsameness.* The confirmation is accomplished on the basis of the being's showing itself ... To say that an assertion *is true* signifies that it uncovers the being as it is

[37] *Ibid.*, pp. 216–217: "Ist es Zufall dass dieses Problem seit mehr denn zwei Jahrtausenden nicht von der Stelle kommt?"

[38] *Ibid.*, p. 217: "Liegt die Verkehrung der Frage schon im Ansatz, in der ontologisch ungeklärten Trennung des Realen und Idealen?"

[39] *Ibid.:* "Und was wird durch die Wahrnehmung ausgewiesen?"

[40] *Ibid.:* "Nichts anders als *dass* es das Seiende selbst *ist,* das in der Aussage gemeint war."

in itself. Such an assertion asserts, points out, "lets" the entity "be seen" in its disclosedness (*Entdecktheit*). The assertion's *being-true* (*truth*) must be understood as being-in-a-state-of-uncovering (entdeckendsein).[41]

It may be instructive to remember once again that the duality of truth, epistemological and ontological, occupied Heidegger's thought almost from the period immediately after the publication of *Being and Time*, 1927, until 1947: "The publication [on Nietzsche] when reflected upon as a whole, ought to offer an insight into the path of thought which I have travelled from 1930 to the *Letter on Humanism* (1947). For the two small lectures, *Plato's Theory of Truth* (1942) and *On the Essence of Truth* (1943), which were published during the aforesaid period, were already conceived during the years 1930–'31."[42] Heidegger's early concern with "truth" apparently led to a step backward in the history of metaphysics, from Aristotle to Plato, in locating the "decisive" stages in man's forgetfulness of Being, through the transformation of ontological into epistemological truth.

Before Plato, Heidegger maintains, truth was experienced as the presence of what appeared, as the unconcealment of beings in Being. Being appears, before Plato, as a quality which is both concealed and revealed in the presence of beings: "Because concealment pervades the nature of Being as a self-concealment for the Greeks, and thus determines beings in their presence and accessibility ('truth'), the Greek word for that which the Romans called 'veritas' and we call 'Wahrheit' is designated by the *a – privative* (*a – létheia*)."[43] The a-privative mediates a negative phenomenon (*léthe, lanthano*), and

---

[41] *Ibid.*: "Diese bewahrt sich darin, dass sich das Ausgesagte, das ist das Seiende selbst, *als dasselbe* zeigt. Bewahrung bedeutet: *sich zeigen des Seienden in Selbigkeit* . . . Die Aussage *ist wahr*, bedeutet: sie entdeckt das Seiende an ihm selbst. Sie sagt aus, sie zeigt auf, sie 'lässt sehen' das Seiende in seiner Entdecktheit. *Wahrsein* (*Wahrheit*) der Aussage muss verstanden werden als *entdeckendsein.*"

[42] *Nietzsche,* vol. I, (Pfullingen, 1961), p. 10: "Die Veröffentlichung möchte, als Ganzes nachgedacht, zugleich einen Blick auf den Denkweg verschaffen, den ich seit 1930 bis zum *Brief über den Humanismus* (1947) gegangen bin. Denn die zwei kleinen, während der genannte Zeit gedruckten Vorträge *Platons Lehre von der Wahrheit* (1942) und *Vom Wesen der Wahrheit* (1943) sind bereits in den Jahren 1930/31 entstanden."

[43] *Platons Lehre von der Wahrheit* (A. Franke: Bern, 1947), p. 25: "Weil für die Griechen anfänglich die Verborgenheit als ein Sichverbergen das Wesen des Seins durchwaltet und somit auch das Seiende in seiner Anwesenheit und Zuganglichkeit ("Wahrheit") bestimmt, deshalb ist das Wort der Griechen für das, was die Römer 'veritas' und wir 'Wahrheit' nennen, durch das *a* privatum (a – letheia) ausgezeichnet."

expresses non-concealment, unhiddenness, non-forgetfulness (re-collection). It is worth noting, in passing, that the essential features of ontological truth, as discussed in *Being and Time,* here form the skeletal structure for Heidegger's critique of Plato. The Greeks, before Plato, presumably understood truth (*alétheia*) as "being-in-a-state-of-uncovering." To the extent that concealment (being-covered, hidden, undisclosed) permeates beings, the truth un-covers, discloses, beings in their un-concealment. Only the terms of the argument shift in two decades: In *Being and Time* truth, in its primordial sense, meant *Entdecktsein* (being-disclosed); in Heidegger's subsequent critique of Plato, the primordial sense of truth means *alétheia,* being unconcealed. Common to both conceptions is the view that beings are fundamentally covered-up, concealed, hidden, as to their Being, and that truth sets them free to *be* in the manner of a disclosure – an "unconcealment." The epistemological sense of truth, in contrast with the ontological sense which suggests the disclosure of beings in their Being, is concerned with the relationship of perception to what is perceived, judgment to object, idea to representation: "non-concealment is *alétheia* in Greek, which is translated as 'truth.' And, for Western thought, 'truth' has for a long time meant the agreement between thought's representation and thing: *adequatio intellectus et rei.*"[44] The suggestion that truth has been conceived as a correspondence between concept and representation in Western thought will, when so flatly stated, appear objectionable to almost any historian of philosophy. It will doubtless be argued that the correspondence theory of truth represents but one sense in which truth has been conceived, beside which one would have to place the coherence and pragmatic theories, at a minimum. In regarding the entire tradition as correspondence oriented, Heidegger would probably collapse such distinctions as derivative. He is not unaware of possible objections which could be raised by historians of philosophy. It is simply that Heidegger uses the concept of agreement, correspondence (*Übereinstimmung*), in a broader sense, which includes all kinds of "agreement;" idea to thing, thing to consistently related ideas, and ideas to their verifiable (or discernible) consequences.

---

[44] *Ibid.,* p. 26: "Unverborgenheit heisst griechisch *aletheia,* welches wort man mit 'Wahrheit' übersetzt. Und 'Wahrheit' bedeutet für das abendländische Denken seit langer Zeit die Übereinstimmung des denkenden Vorstellens mit der Sache: adequatio intellectus et rei."

In ascribing an embryonic form of the correspondence theory to Plato, Heidegger acknowledges that "The interpretation threatens to degenerate into a forced reinterpretation," but quickly adds: "This appears to be the case until our insight has secured that what underlies Plato's thinking is a change in the essence of truth, which becomes the hidden law of what he says as a thinker." [45] Whether or not proceeding from a "hidden law" – from what a thinker does not say – is methodologically sound is not at issue at this point. It must be remembered that the reflection on Plato is not an historical-philosophical interpretation employing conventional scholarly tools. It is guided and determined by the question of the meaning of Being. Heidegger defines what he means by Plato's "doctrine" of truth, the subject of his interpretation as follows: "The 'doctrine' of a thinker is that which is left unsaid in what he says." [46] Apparently, what is presupposed but unexpressed in Plato's allegory of the cave is a transformation in the meaning and dimension of *alétheia*.

In the stages of the soul's turning to the light (allegory of the cave) Plato de-emphasizes disclosure (*alétheia*) itself, Heidegger maintains. Principal attention is no longer devoted to the phenomenon of non-concealment, the disclosure of beings in Being. Non-concealment is subordinated to that which is revealed, and the manner in which it is perceived. *Alétheia* becomes instrumental in revealing the Forms, by preparing their visibility for sight. What assumes increasing importance in Plato's "doctrine" is that the Forms shine forth in unconcealment, and that they be correctly viewed. With the dominance of *idea* over *alétheia* the central problem becomes that of right vision of the Form (the *idein* of the *idea*). *Alétheia* gradually begins to assume the character of *orthotes*, of *correctness* of apprehension. The correctness of sight in relation to what is sighted (the *orthotes* of *idein* to *idea*) guarantees *homoiosis* – a "correspondence" between knowledge and its object.

The transition from one context to another consists in vision's becoming more correct. Everything depends on the *orthotes*, on the correctness of vision. Through this correctness seeing and knowing are made right . . . In this self-directing, perception is compared with that which is to be

[45] *Ibid.*, p. 25: "Die Auslegung droht in eine gewaltsame Umdeutung auszuarten. Mag dies so scheinen, bis sich die Einsicht gefestigt hat, dass Platons Denken sich einem Wandel des Wesens der Wahrheit unterwirft, der zum verborgenen Gesetz dessen wird, was der Denker sagt."

[46] *Ibid.*, p. 5: "Die 'Lehre' eines Denkers ist das in seinem Sagen Ungesagte."

sighted. This is the "appearance" of beings. As a consequence of this
assimilation of perception as an *idein* to an *idea,* a *homoiosis* remains, a
correspondence between knowledge and the thing itself. And so, out of
the foreground of *idea* and *idein* a change in the nature of truth springs
forth before *aletheia.* Truth becomes *orthotes,* correctness of perception
and expression.

In this transformation in the nature of truth a change in the location of
truth is simultaneously affected. As nonconcealment truth is still a fundamental feature of beings themselves. As correctness of "vision," however, it becomes the designation of man's relationship to beings.[47]

The change in the nature of truth to which Heidegger refers, has
been characterized, here, as a transformation of ontological truth into
epistemological truth. Epistemological truth, as a correspondence
between idea and representation, is but one mode of truth, according
to Heidegger. Truth, conceived as *alétheia,* is revealed in a plenitude
of modes. Truth, conceived as correctness, finds its negation only in
falsehood, error – when the idea fails to represent what it claims. Ontological truth, on the other hand, wrests the presence of beings from
their multiple concealments: ". . . there can be many types of concealment: enclosing, hoarding, disguising, covering-up, dissimu-
lating."[48] As far as Heidegger is concerned, "The nature of truth
surrenders the basic feature of unconcealment"[49] after Plato. After
Plato metaphysics conceives truth as essentially a relationship of
knower to known, rather than as a quality of beings. Hence, in finding
the traditional criteria of Being – universality, undefinability, and
self-evidence – inadequate, Heidegger criticizes them as heirs of the

---

[47] *Ibid.,* pp. 41–42: "Der Übergang von einer Lage in die andere besteht in
dem Richtigerwerden des Blickens. An der *orthotes,* der Richtigkeit des Blickens,
liegt alles. Durch diese Richtigkeit wird das Sehen und Erkennen ein rechtes . . .
In diesem Sichrichten gleicht sich das Vernehmen dem an, was gesichtet sein
soll. Das ist das 'Aussehen' des Seienden. Zufolge dieser Angleichung des Vernehmens als eines *idein* an die *idea* besteht eine *homoiosis,* eine Übereinstimmung des Erkennens mit der Sache selbst. So entspringt aus dem Vorrang der
idea und des *idein* vor der *aletheia* eine Wandlung des Wesens der Wahrheit.
Wahrheit wird zur *orthotes,* zur Richtigkeit des Vernehmens und Aussagens.
In diesem Wandel des Wesens der Wahrheit vollzieht sich zugleich ein Wechsel des Ortes der Wahrheit. Als Unverborgenheit ist sie noch ein Grundzug des
Seienden selbst. Als Richtigkeit des 'Blickens' aber wird sie zur Auszeichnung
des menschlichen Verhaltens zum Seienden."

[48] *Ibid.,* p. 32: "Die Verborgenheit kann dabei verschiedener Art sein: Ver-
schliessung, Verwahrung, Verhüllung, Verdeckung, Verschleierung, Verstel-
lung."

[49] *Ibid.,* p. 41: "Das Wesen der Wahrheit gibt den Grundzug der Unverborgenheit preis."

epistemological concept of truth. The criteria treat Being as another being, of which we can say that it is undefinable, universal and self-evident.

The phenomenon of truth, then, is intimately connected with Being. It should be added that Heidegger regards what we have called the epistemological concept of truth as humanistic. It is "humanistic" in so far as it makes truth dependent upon man, explicitly or implicitly, in his dealings with beings. Truth, as a quality of beings in *their* presence, is allegedly veiled and obscured.

Heidegger's reflections on Plato's "doctrine" of truth are of more than passing interest to us, because he tends to identify the epistemological truth orientation as "metaphysical" and dominant in Western thought. It follows, for Heidegger, that the metaphysical-humanistic standpoint is incapable of discovering Being, that it veils, obscures, and dissimulates it through the domination of epistemological (Platonic) truth. "From now on the mold of the nature of truth, as the correctness of representing through assertion, becomes decisive for all Western thought." [50]

Whatever else may be said about the value of Heidegger's interpretation of Plato, it should be kept in mind that it is inescapably connected with the search for the meaning of Being, and its attempted retrieval. Heidegger was persuaded, before 1927, that Being had fallen into oblivion in Western metaphysics. His guiding question then became how this event occurred and on what occasion. And, in answer to both questions, it occurred with Plato, through the subordination of truth, *alétheia,* to the Forms (*eidos, idea*). Heidegger charged Plato with subjectivizing truth by locating its nature in *orthotes* and *logos.* The phenomenon of truth no longer centers on non-concealment, after Plato, but centers, implicitly, on certitude instead.

It is of some importance to observe, once again, that Heidegger's plans as stated in *Being and Time* have been altered. Whereas Kant, Descartes, and Aristotle, were considered "decisive" phases in the retrogressive evolution of the question of Being in that work, Plato and Nietzsche assume prominent roles for the later Heidegger. This is due to the fact that Heidegger increasingly stressed the interrelationship of the Being-question and the theory of truth. The division

---

[50] *Ibid.,* p. 44: "Von nun an wird das Gepräge des Wesens der Wahrheit als der Richtigkeit des aussagenden Vorstellens massgebend für das gesamte abendländische Denken."

between Being and truth (*alétheia*) becomes blurred in the work of
the later Heidegger, as Plato and Nietzsche assume increasing importance for the problem of truth.

Heidegger's apparently simplistic claims about Greek philosophy,
medieval philosophy, and modern philosophy are all based, in my
judgment, on the contention that the epistemological truth concept
has dominated the tradition and has, as a result, transformed Being
into simply another – although "special" – being. Due to the connection between Being and truth, Heidegger finds it adequate to cite
quotations which he takes as evidence of the epistemological truth
criterion within each period of philosophy, to support his view of the
devolution of Being.

As evidence of this it is sufficient to cite the principal propositions
which are characteristic of the perpetual molding of the nature of truth
within the principal ages of metaphysics.
A statement of St. Thomas Aquinas holds true for Medieval Scholastic-
ism: *Veritas proprie invenitur in intellectu humano vel divino* (Quaestiones
de veritate; qu. 1 art. 4, resp.), "truth is really encountered in the human
or in the divine understanding." It has its essential place in the understanding. Here truth is no longer *alétheia* but *homoiosis (adequatio)*.
At the beginning of the modern age Descartes sharpens the above
quotation by saying: *veritatem proprie vel falsitatem non nisi in solo intellectu esse posse (Regulae ad directionem ingenii;* Reg. VII, Opp. X,
396). "Truth or falsehood in the genuine sense cannot be anywhere else
except in the understanding alone." [51]

The movement from Plato to Descartes represents an intensification, a sharpening, of the epistemological criterion of truth and the
attending devolution of Being, due, in part, to its conceptualization.
The movement is one phase of the history of Being, in which truth

---

[51] *Ibid.,* pp. 44–45: "Zum Zeugnis dafür diene und genüge die Anführung
der Leitsätze, die in den Hauptzeitaltern der Metaphysik die jeweilige Prägung
des Wesens der Wahrheit kennzeichnen.
"Für die mittelalterliche Scholastik gilt der Satz des Thomas v. A.: veritas
proprie invenitur in intellectu humano del divino (Quaestiones de veritate; qu. I
art. 4, resp.), 'die Wahrheit wird eigentlich angetroffen im menschlichen oder
im göttlichen Verstand.' Im Verstand hat sie ihren Wesensort. Wahrheit ist hier
nicht mehr *aletheia,* sondern *homoiosis* (adequatio).
"Am Beginn der Neuzeit sagt Descartes in einer Verschärfung des vorigen
Satzes: veritatem proprie vel falsitatem non nisi in solo intellectu esse posse
(Regulae ad directionem ingenii, Reg. VIII, Opp. X, 396). 'Wahrheit oder Falsch-
heit im eigentlichen Sinne können nirgendwo anders denn allein im Verstande
sein.' "

becomes certitude, in which Being and truth both lose the quality of unhiddenness. Moreover, Descartes' intensification of a tendency implicit in Plato constitutes the rise of modern subjectivism. That is, in Plato a human criterion for truth is implicitly substituted for an ontological one. This becomes fully explicit in Descartes, in so far as the *cogito* becomes the point of reference for the meaning of beings.

This also distinguishes "modern" from "medieval" man. To be sure man also had a privileged place in creation in the medieval panorama. However, beings were still understood, by most Scholastics, in terms of their relationship to a creating God. With Descartes all ontological grounds for certitude vanish. William Richardson states the matter succinctly when he says – for Heidegger – that with Descartes "only that is true which can be verified in a manner analogous to the knowing sub-ject's certitude of itself, sc. by guaranteeing the conformity between presentation and presented. All beings have sense, then, sc. 'are,' only in terms of the subject-object relationship . . ." [52]

The hasty sketch thus far presented in this chapter merely serves to indicate Heidegger's attitude toward the tradition. Each phase of the historical development of truth and Being needs further elboration, qualification and, of course, critical scrutiny. Such an undertaking would take us outside the scope of our present inquiry, however.

This restriction notwithstanding, one cannot ignore the fact that even the general *context* which informs Heidegger's Nietzsche interpretation is historically inaccurate. First, in Heidegger's "reconstruction" of the basic views of his predecessors, his exclusive emphasis distorts their teachings. Thus, for example, the interpretation of Plato's doctrine as the implicit devolution of *alétheia* into *orthotes,* and the ensuing treatment of Being as *a* being, is highly questionable. The claims about Descartes fare no better. Second, if the epistemological truth concept is "humanistic," dependent upon man and hence incapable of revealing Being, the same "humanistic" truth criterion pervades Heidegger's own *Being and Time*. Third, and last, the suggestion that truth has, at bottom, always meant some version of *adequatio intellectus et rei,* and that philosophers have traditionally presupposed such a truth-concept, is simply false. To point out the his-

---

[52] William Richardson, *Heidegger: Through Phenomenology to Thought* (Martinus Nijhoff, The Hague, 1963), p. 330.

torical inaccuracy of such a claim one need only turn, quite briefly, to Hegel, who addresses himself directly to the inadequacy of such a concept of truth.

With regard to the first criticism, it should be pointed out that Plato's alleged subordination of *alétheia* to *orthotes* expresses a half-truth (however interesting and suggestive such a half-truth may be). I am reminded of a story which one of Heidegger's most sympathetic commentators, William Richardson, told when he delivered the 1965 "Suarez Lecture" at Fordham University.[53] When confronted with the history of criticisms of his interpretation of Kant, Heidegger simply said; it may not be good Kant, but it's excellent Heidegger. I think substantially the same comment can be made, substituting for the word "Kant," the words "Plato," or "Descartes," or "history of philosophy." In the case of Plato, the suggestion that "truth" somehow falls under the yoke of the forms *eidos, idea* (by becoming the instrument for selecting the "correct" *logos* which agrees with the form), misses the mark. In the section which immediately precedes the allegory of the cave, the divided line,[54] Plato concludes by pointing out that the various levels of intellection are clear and certain according to the degree of truth and reality *the objects of intellection* possess: "Assigning to each level of intellection a degree of clearness and certainty corresponding to the measure in which their objects possess truth and reality." [55] Clearly the philosopher-king's discerning gaze is not made "right" merely by *corresponding* to its object, for this would be "true" also of opinion; *doxa*. The "rightness" of cognition is determined by something which is antecedently real; namely, the object *in its truth*. In a non-Heideggerian context, Plato's vision is surely guided by "true Being." That is, after all, what the Platonic ascent to the forms is all about. How can the ontologically prior form of the Good (*auto to agathon*) be in any sense "humanistic?" Truth, after all, is guided by, accords with, what truly *is*. The "accord" alone does not define truth. The accord must agree with what truly *is* the case, it must reveal the "object" in a state of *unconcealment* (*alétheia*). Philo-

---

[53] Richardson, having just returned from Freiburg to accept the invitation to speak, with Heidegger's approval, on the topic "Heidegger and God," elected instead to defend Heidegger against certain accusations and criticisms; especially Hans Jonas' charge that Heidegger had implicitly sanctioned Nazism.

[54] *Republic* VI, 511.

[55] *The Republic of Plato,* trans. F. M. Cornford (New York and London: Oxford University Press, 1941), p. 226.

sophic dialectic is designed to lay bare, un-veil, un-cover, un-conceal, what truly *is*, beyond the chimerical cycle of what merely *appears to be*. That which truly *is* appears in a state of unconcealment through the process of the dialectic. Doesn't "truth" here mean, in *addition* to "correctness," something like Heidegger's "being-in-a-state-of-un-covering" (*entdeckendsein*)? Note that when Glaucon asks Socrates to describe the function of philosophic discourse, Socrates does *not* reply that truth can be "correctly" revealed in *logos*: "you will not be able to follow me farther, though not for want of willingness on my part. It would mean that, instead of illustrating the truth by an allegory, I should be showing you the truth itself, at least as it appears to me. I cannot be sure whether or not I see it as it really is; but we can be sure that there is some such reality which it concerns us to see." [56] Truth, *alétheia*, is not merely a matter of selecting the adequate *logos* which correctly identifies a *homoiosis* between itself and its object. *Alétheia,* on the contrary, can only be pointed to in its fullness "by an allegory." The reality of truth for Plato, then, resides not only in the "judgment," but in the ontologically prior datum to which all knowledge addresses itself.

Heidegger's reading of Descartes is, it seems to me, equally questionable. Quoting the assertion that "truth or falsehood in the genuine sense cannot be anywhere else except in the understanding alone" [57] will not generate, by itself, the kind of subjectivism Heidegger has in mind. William Richardson quite correctly spells out the consequences Heidegger attaches to Descartes' role in the history of metaphysics. By locating truth in the understanding "only that is true which can be verified in a manner analogous to the knowing sub-jects certitude of itself, sc. by guaranteeing the conformity between presentation and presented. All beings have sense, then sc. 'are,' only in terms of the subject-object relationship." [58] Although it may be true that, for Descartes, truth – "in the genuine sense" – exists in the understanding alone, truth is *guaranteed* neither by the subject nor the subject's self-certainty. Truth is guaranteed by the "natural light," by intuition, which, in turn, is guaranteed by God.

---

[56] *Ibid.,* p. 253.

[57] *Platons Lehre von der Wahrheit* (A. Franke: Bern, 1947), p. 45.

[58] William Richardson, *Heidegger: Through Phenomenology to Thought* (Martinus Nijhoff: The Hague, 1963), p. 330.

By *intuition* I understand, not the fluctuating testimony of the senses, nor the misleading judgment that proceeds from the blundering constructions of imagination, but the conception which an unclouded and attentive mind gives us so readily and distinctly that we are wholly freed from doubt about that which we understand. Or, what comes to the same thing, *intuition* is the undoubting conception of an unclouded (*purae*) and attentive mind, and springs from the light of reason alone.[59]

Descartes is clearly *not* dealing with two regions of entities alone and their relation; "understanding" and "beings." It is simply mistaken to assert that beings "are," for Descartes, in virtue of their being verified "in a manner analogous to the knowing subjects certitude of itself."[60] Such an interpretation confuses method and result, methodological priority and ontological priority. Ontologically, Descartes leaves the cosmos lamentably well intact. God is *first,* the world *is* second, the *cogito is* third. Methodologically, however, since one can doubt the existence of God, the world, and one's body (through the interchangeability of the waking and dreaming state), the only *first* indubitable starting point is *cogito ergo sum.* The *res cogitans* exists because its necessary existence is clear to the natural light of reason. "Thus each individual can mentally have intuition of the fact that he exists, and that he thinks."[61] When Descartes asserts that truth, "in the genuine sense," is really encountered in the understanding alone, it is important to recognize the meaning of "in the genuine sense." Heidegger's quotation, taken from Descartes, completely ignores the context in which it arises. For the sake of historical accuracy, Descartes locates truth in the understanding *as opposed to imagination and sensation:*

he will enumerate among other things whatever instruments of thought we have other than the understanding; and these are only two, viz., imagination and sense. He will therefore devote all his energies to the distinguishing and examining of these three modes of cognition, and seeing that in the strict, [i.e. "genuine"] sense truth and falsity can be a matter of the understanding alone ,though often it derives its origin from the other two faculties, he will attend carefully to every source of deception in order that he may be on his guard.[62]

---

[59] *The Philosophical Works of Descartes,* Vol. I, transl. Haldane and Ross (Dover Publication, 1955), p. 7: "Rules for the Direction of the Mind."

[60] William Richardson, *Heidegger: Through Phenomenology to Thought,* p. 330.

[61] *The Philosophical Works of Descartes,* transl. Haldane and Ross, p. 7.

[62] *Ibid.,* p. 25.

The above quotation, then, is not an ontological claim which may be interpreted to mean beings "are" if and only if they satisfy, correspond to, the truth as defined by the understanding. Heidegger's quotation cited from this passage ["Truth or falsehood in the genuine sense cannot be anywhere else except in the understanding alone" [63]] expresses a *methodological* directive, not an ontological principle. If we want to know, i.e., be certain, about what exists, we should guard against the sources of deception, viz., imagination and the testimony of then senses. There is a distinction between asserting "beings have sense, then sc. 'are,' only in terms of the subject-object relationship" [64] and asserting "we *know* that beings 'are' only in terms of the subject-object relationship." Descartes' quotation implies the latter, the epistemic claim, not the former – the ontological claim. In collapsing this distinction, Richardson, although faithful to Heidegger's intention, distorts Descartes' meaning. Moreover, I think it is not unfair to suggest that by taking a part of a sentence out of context, as Heidegger does with Descartes, and interpreting it as the *basis* of a philosopher's position, one can "demonstrate" virtually anything.

With regard to the second general criticism of Heidegger's view of the tradition, that the "truth" criterion he rejects pervades his own *Being and Time,* one need not select sentences out of context to demonstrate this point. The entire critical discussion of the *Kehre,* the reversal in Heidegger's thinking, centers on the sudden transformation from a Daseinsanalysis to a Being-analysis.

In *Being and Time,* Dasein was conceived as a being-in-the-world, where its Being *and* the world's are reciprocally disclosed. Consequently, Heidegger asserts "Of course, only as long as Dasein is (that is, only as long as an understanding of Being is ontically possible), 'is there' Being. When Dasein does not exist, 'independence' 'is' not either, nor 'is' the 'in-itself.' In that case even beings within-the-world can neither be disclosed nor lie concealed. *Then* it cannot be said that beings are, nor can it be said that they are not." [65] Without the exis-

---

[63] *Platons Lehre von der Wahrheit,* p. 45.

[64] William Richardson, *Heidegger: Through Phenomenology to Thought,* p. 330.

[65] *Sein und Zeit,* p. 212: "Allerdings nur solange Dasein *ist,* das heisst die ontische Möglichkeit von Seinsverständnis, 'gibt es' Sein. Wenn Dasein nicht existiert, dann 'ist' auch nicht 'Unabhängigkeit' und 'ist' auch nicht 'Ansich' . . . Dann ist auch innerweltliches Seiendes weder entdeckbar, noch kann es in Verborgenheit liegen. Dann kann weder gesagt werden, dass Seiendes sei, noch dass es nicht sei."

tence of Dasein, this quotation seems to assert, disclosure (truth), beings, and Being "are" not either. I select the phrase "seems to assert," because Heidegger evidently does not want to interpret his passage in that way. When critics were profoundly disturbed by Heidegger's post-*Being and Time* reversal of perspective, which seems to assert the "independence" of Being and man's dependence upon it, and pointed to the above passage as evidence of the interdependence of Being, truth, and man, Heidegger replied: "In *Being and Time* (p. 212) it is said intentionally and cautiously: *il y a l'Etre*: 'it gives' Being. The *il y a* translates the 'it gives' inexactly. For the 'it,' which here 'gives,' is Being itself. The 'gives' names, however, the essence of Being; the giving itself and the imparting of its truth. The giving itself into the open with this self, is Being itself."[66] This remarkable self-interpretation simply translates the German idiom, "*es gibt*" (there is), literally; *es* (it) *gibt* (gives). In consequence, Heidegger insists that the passage in question should be read to mean "Of course only as long as Dasein is (that is, only as long as an understanding of Being is ontically possible) does Being 'give itself'."[67] It is extremely odd, if this indeed was Heidegger's intention, that his following sentence drops the idiomatic "*es gibt*" altogether, and asserts that without Dasein "independence" and "in-itselfness" – precisely the "categories" later suggested for "self-giving" Being – do not exist (*existieren*)! "When Dasein does not exist (*existiert*), 'independence' 'is' ('*ist*') not either, nor 'is' ('*ist*') the 'in-itself'."[68] If, indeed, "es gibt" was supposed to mean "it gives" rather than "there is," why wasn't the self-granting sense of "independent" Being retained in the next sentence? The lengths to which Heidegger will go in re-interpreting his own *magnum opus* to make it consistent with the "non-humanistic" standpoint of his later work is distressing. In an effort to show the initial priority of Being, Heidegger says,

But it is not said in *Being and Time* (p. 212), where "it gives" finds expression, that "only as long as Dasein is, is there Being?" Certainly. This

---

[66] *Platons Lehre von der Wahrheit: mit einem Brief über den "Humanismus"* (Franke: Bern, 1947), p. 80: "In 'S. u. Z.: (S. 212) ist mit Absicht und Vorsicht gesagt: il y a l'Etre: 'es gibt' das Sein. Das il y a übersetzt das 'es gibt' ungenau. Denn das 'es," was hier 'gibt,' ist das Sein selbst. Das 'gibt' nennt jedoch das gebende, seine Wahrheit gewährende Wesen des Seins. Das Sichgeben ins Offene mit diesem selbst ist das Sein selber."

[67] *Sein und Zeit*, p. 212. cf. note 65 for German.

[68] *Ibid.*

means: only as long as the clearing of Being is realized, is Being itself conveyed to man. That the "there" (*Da*), however, that the clearing of Being itself is realized, is the destiny of Being itself. This is the destiny of the clearing. The sentence, however, does not mean that the Dasein of man in the traditional sense of *existentia*, understood in the modern period (*neuzeitlich*) as the actuality of the *ego cogito,* would be the being through which alone Being is created. The sentence does not say that Being is a product of man. The introduction to *Being and Time* (p. 38) states simply and clearly and even in italics that "Being is the *transcendens* as such." [69]

Heidegger's attempt to re-inforce the interpretation that, to put it simply, Dasein is dependent upon Being even in *Being and Time,* stresses the view that Being was initially conceived as "*transcendens*" as such. However, if one does turn to the introduction to *Being and Time,* in which the term "transcendens" is introduced, two very distinct conceptions of "transcendens" emerge. The first meaning of "transcendens" is associated with the criterion of "universiality" and is rejected: "The 'universiality' of Being 'transcends' any universality of genus. In medieval ontology 'Being' is designated as '*transcendens*' ... So if it said that 'Being' is the most universal concept, this cannot mean that it is one which is clearest and in no further need of discussion." [70] In the context of Heidegger's initial critique of metaphysics (*Being and Time*), any reification of Being – a "transcendens" stemming from the universality of Being – belongs to the tradition of *Seinsvergessenheit,* the forgetfulness of Being. Thus, when Heidegger finally says "*Being is transcendens pure and simple,*" [71] he does *not*

[69] *Platons Lehre von der Wahrheit,* p. 83: "Aber ist nicht in 'S.u.Z.' (S. 212), wo das 'es gibt' zur Sprache kommt, gesagt: 'Nur solange Dasein ist, gibt es Sein?' Allerdings. Das bedeutet: nur solange die Lichtung des Seins sich ereignet, übereignet sich Sein dem Menschen. Dass aber das Da, die Lichtung als Wahrheit des Seins selbst, sich ereignet, ist die Schickung des Seins selbst. Dieses ist das Geschick der Lichtung. Der Satz bedeutet aber nicht: das Dasein des Menschen im überlieferten Sinne von existentia, und neuzeitlich gedacht als die Wirklichkeit des ego cogito, sei dasjenige Seiende, wodurch das Sein erst geschaffen werde. Der Satz sagt nicht, das Sein sei ein Produkt des Menschen. In der Einleitung zu 'S.u.Z.' (S. 38) steht einfach und klar und sogar im Sperrdruck: 'Sein ist das transzendens schlechthin.'"

[70] *Sein und Zeit,* p. 3: "Die 'allgemeinheit' des Seins '*übersteigt*' alle gattungsmässige Allgemeinheit. 'Sein' ist nach der Bezeichnung der mittelalterlichen Ontologie ein 'transcendens' ... Wenn man demnach sagt: 'Sein' ist der allgemeinste Begriff, so kann das nicht heissen, er ist der klarste und aller weiteren Erörterung unbedürftig."

[71] *Ibid.,* p. 38: "*Sein ist das transcendens schlechthin.*"

mean a self-granting, self-giving Being. The "transcendens" of Being is cited there in explicit opposition to any reified independently transcendent "Being." The sentences which immediately follow the assertion that "Being is transcendens," make it clear that transcendence is still understood in the context of Dasein's self-disclosure: "And the transcendence of Dasein's Being is distinctive in that it implies the possibility and the necessity of the most radical *individuation*. Every disclosure of Being as the *transcendens* is *transcendental* knowledge. *Phenomenological truth (the disclosedness of Being) is veritas transcendentalis.*" [72] At the risk of belaboring the point, the reference to "transcendens" in *Being and Time* is *not* a reference to Being, understood in the sense of reified "transcendens" which Heidegger had clearly rejected, but a reference to Being's "transcendens" as transcendental "knowledge" and "truth." The context, then, is "humanistic." It would appear that Heidegger's interpretation of his own *Being and Time* employs the same questionable latitude as does his interpretation of Plato or Descartes.

One point should be noted. By citing the potentially humanistic context of *Being and Time,* we do not infer from this that, somehow, we are free to dispose of Heidegger's critique of the history of metaphysics. The issue was raised only to point out the extent to which the later Heidegger is anxious to free Being from Dasein, from beings, and to free ontological truth from any connection with epistemological truth. In this process, we have argued, Heidegger distorts not only the teachings of past philosophers, but distorts *Being and Time* as well.

The final criticism of Heidegger's approach to the history of philosophy involves what, in our judgment, is too simple a concept of truth:

"Non-concealment is *aletheia* in Greek, which is translated as "truth." And, for Western thought, "truth" has for a long time meant the agreement between thought's representation and thing: *adequatio intellectus et rei . . .*[73]

---

[72] *Ibid:* "Die Transzendenz des Seins des Daseins ist eine ausgezeichnete, sofern in ihr die Möglichkeit und Notwendigkeit der radikalsten *Individuation* liegt. Jede Erschliessung von Sein als des transcendens ist *transcendentale* Erkenntnis. *Phenomenologische Wahrheit (Erschlossenheit von Sein) ist veritas transcendentalis.*"

[73] *Platons Lehre von der Wahrheit,* p. 32: "Unverborgenheit heisst griechisch *aletheia,* welches wort man mit 'Wahrheit' übersetzt. Und 'Wahrheit' bedeutet

According to this opinion, the ideal content of judgment stands in a relationship of agreement. This relationship thus pertains to a connection between an ideal content of judgment and the real thing as that which is judged *about*. Is this agreement real or ideal in its kind of Being, or neither of these? *How is the relationship between ideal being and real being to be grasped ontologically?* . . . Is it accidental that no headway has been made with this problem in over two thousand years.[74]

The two central claims sustaining and informing Heidegger's critique of metaphysics are (1) that truth has traditionally constituted a correspondence between judgment and its object, and (2) that such a truth concept generates an insuperable dichotomy between "ideal" and "real," between the content of a judgment and its object. Moreover, no progress ("headway") has been made in grasping "ontologically" the relationship between the "ideal" content of a judgment and the "real" object to which this content stands in a truth relationship.

Such a normative claim is difficult to criticize because we do not know what Heidegger would admit as evidence of "headway" having been made. But it can be argued that the description of truth as basically an agreement between *intellectus* and *rei* is too narrow to cover "two thousand years" of the history of philosophy.

One need not necessarily be an Hegelian to recognize that one of Hegel's chief problems was an effort to overcome precisely the narrow correspondence view of truth which Heidegger ascribes to the history of metaphysics. Without entering into the interesting complexities of Hegel's philosophy, commentators generally agree on at the least one point, namely, that "truth" meant, for Hegel, the correspondence between an object and *its* concept. However difficult such a concept of truth may be, it issues out of the attempt to get beyond *adequatio intellectus et rei*:

a bad state and a diseased person are contradictory and "untrue" in this sense, as not living up to their concepts. Hegel is careful to say that such contradictory "untruth" has nothing to do with the correctness of the judgments describing the corrupt condition of such objects. The con-

für das abendländische Denken seit langer Zeit die Übereinstimmung des denkenden Vorstellens mit der Sache: adequatio intellectus et rei."

[74] *Sein und Zeit,* pp. 216–217: "Diese betrifft sonach einen Zusammenhang zwischen idealem Urteilsgehalt und dem realen Ding als dem worüber geurteilt wird. Ist das Übereinstimmen seiner Seinsart nach real oder ideal oder keines von beiden? *Wie soll die Beziehung zwischen idealen Seiendem und real Vorhandenem ontologisch gefasst* werden? . . . Ist es Zufall, dass dieses Problem seit mehr denn zwei Jahrtausenden nicht von der Stelle kommt?"

formity of our notion to the object (correctness) is quite different from the conformity of the object to its *own* notion ("truth). Here it is plain that Hegel is using the predicates "contradictory" and "untrue" in a manner quite different from other logicians and philosophers . . .[75]

A judgment is "true" in proportion as the moments distinguished in it coincide in their content, in proportion as they represent the conformity of a thing to its notion. In proportion as they fall short of such coincidence, judgments will be more and more untrue, though Hegel does not question that they may be right (*richtig*), that they may agree with their objects and set forth their state correctly.[76]

Albert Hofstadter's recent book, *Truth and Art*,[77] focuses, in part, on the nature of the relationship between *intellectus* and *rei*, and states the problem this way.

In speaking of he mutual adequation of intellect and thing, the formula of truth requires a two-way conformity. There must be in this truth (1) something of the nature of an uncovering or truth of understanding, like the truth of statement, and (2) something of the nature of a governance, i.e. something like a thing-truth, practical truth, or truth of will. And (3) these cannot be unrelated to each other. If intellect and thing are mutually adequated, then the intellect, in uncovering the thing, must at the same time be governing the thing; and again, in governing the thing the intellect must at the same time be uncovering the thing.[78]

The first two distinctions introduced by Hofstadter reveal two senses of *adequatio*, with two corresponding senses of truth. When a judgment "agrees" with its object, is guided by and uncovers its object in its self-sameness, the "truth" is propositional ("truth of statement," in Albert Hofstadter's usage). In this case the *adequatio* is an *adequatio intellectus ad rei*. But the reverse adequation, *adequatio rei ad intellectus*, is also a possible way in which a "conformity" between understanding and thing may arise. When the thing adequately conforms to *our* "idea" of it, the locus of truth changes. Such "truth" is called "truth of things" by Hofstadter. "Performative" utterances, afford an excellent example:

. . . a religious official having gone through the proper form of the marriage ceremony, concludes, "I pronounce you man and wife." In this pronouncement he is not merely reporting the fact of his pronouncing.

---

[75] J. N. Findlay. *Hegel: A Re-Examination* (New York: Collier Books, 1962), p. 63.

[76] *Ibid.,* p. 232.

[77] Albert Hofstadter, *Truth and Art* (New York and London: Columbia University Press, 1965).

[78] *Ibid.,* pp. 130–131.

There is, of course, a statemental element in it; he is indeed reporting what he is doing, but this is only part of his meaning. His pronouncement is not just an autobiographical datum. He is executing a religious-legal act of permission, sanctification, and binding obligation upon the couple. In his pronouncement he announces a change in their religious, legal, and social status, subjecting them to a complex of rights and duties, being empowered to do so by his office and doing so in the context of the correct procedure of the ceremony as determined by the religious-legal code. The function of the pronouncement, then, is just to announce this change of status. *Qua* pronouncement it is the institutive announcement of the condition of marriage between the two persons united. This instituting or establishing in announcing is its function and mode of being . . . Thus the thing-truth of this pronouncement is defined in terms of the ought provided by the law.[79]

Although we do not, conventionally, assign a "truth" function to ceremonial language, the important point for us is that the "two-way conformity" of "idea" to "thing" and "thing" to "idea" requires a higher resolution. As it stands, the duality of truth – "truth of statement" and "truth of things" – still falls within the sphere of what we have called "epistemological" truth. Heidegger would doubtless suggest that the "two" concepts of truth still do not resolve the dilemma of the relationship between "ideal" content and "real" thing. The only change introduced by the second truth relationship is that the *conformity* changes. The "real" thing must conform to the "ideal" content of the judgment; not only must the "ideal" content conform to the thing. Aware of this difficulty Hofstadter introduces a third dimension of truth, "truth of spirit," which is – in its essential features – derived from Hegel and Schelling: "But this language, borrowed from the two previous concepts of truth, is only provisional; for it would be just as true to say that it is the thing that uncovers the intellect and the thing that governs the intellect. The concept that is identical in intention with the thing, in the act of uncovering the thing, must at the same time, in the act of governing, be the concept that the thing identically realizes in being as it ought to be."[80] It is this third concept of truth, implying a conformity of the object to its *own* concept, and the intellect's dependence upon such an adequation for its truth, which Hegel had attempted to work out. As Albert Hofstadter rightly suggests, this third kind of truth lies at the foundation of Hegel's system.

[79] *Ibid.*, pp. 115–116.
[80] *Ibid.*, p. 131.

The third kind of truth, therefore, is in the first place an *objective* occurrence of truth, on which the *subjective* realization of thought and will depend secondarily. This is pointed out by Hegel in his estimation of the relation of truth to existence or reality. "A thing that appears is not true by the fact that it has an inner or an outer existence, and is in general a reality, but only by the fact that this reality corresponds to the concept. Only then does the existent thing have actuality and truth. And, indeed, truth not in the *subjective* sense, that an existent shows itself to be in conformity with *my* representation, but in the *objective* sense, that the ego or an external object, action, event, state, realizes in its actuality the concept itself. If this identity does not come about, then the existent thing is merely an appearance." (*Sämmtliche Werke*, 12, 159–160).[81]

At another point, clarifying once again this third sense of truth, Hegel says:

Truth in the deeper sense consists in the identity between objectivity and the notion. It is in this deeper sense that we speak of a true state, or of a true work of art. These objects are true, if they are as they ought to be, i.e., if their reality corresponds with their notion. When thus viewed, to be untrue means much the same as to be bad. A bad man is an untrue man, a man who does not behave as his notion or his vocation requires.[82]

In the light of the preceding quotations from Hegel, we feel justified in concluding that Heidegger's claims that no "headway" has been made in over two thousand years in our understanding of the *adequatio intellectus et rei* is unjustified.

The three criticisms of Heidegger's view of the history of philosophy developed here (namely; that he inaccurately describes the teachings of his predecessors, that he inaccurately interprets his own *Being and Time*, and that his epistemological truth criterion unjustifiably restricts the manifold ways in which truth has been "traditionally" understood, as, for example, in Hegel) have not been raised in a spirit of rejection. We do not imply that Heidegger's reading of the history of metaphysics is invalid nonsense. Rather, we wanted to show that his interpretation is subordinated to a thesis which superimposes its meaning upon the history of philosophy. As Heidegger himself asserts: "The 'doctrine' of a thinker is that which is left unsaid in what

---

[81] *Ibid.*, p. 138.

[82] *The Logic of Hegel*, transl. William Wallace (London: Oxford University Press, 1931), p. 354.

he says." [83] But the dangers inherent in this method should be recognized. Although it yields a suggestive and partially correct insight into the history of thought, it is not a method to be emulated, for the results are necessarily distortions.

Heidegger's view of the tradition, as has been repeatedly indicated, is informed by the question of Being. That Being had fallen into oblivion was a conviction from which Heidegger began — it is not a conclusion which he reached. The epistemological concept of truth holds within it the tendency to reduce Being to Being-as-understood, hence to *a* being. The epistemological concept of truth also holds within it the tendency to (correctly) assume a human criterion, hence "humanism," as the basis upon which the Being of beings is understood.

Albert Hofstadter is probably correct in ascribing a realist position to Heidegger. Heidegger's dismay over subjectivism and realism missed the mark, Hofstadter suggests, "because he himself presupposes a realist answer to it. Heidegger repudiates the title of realism for his own view, but is able to do this only because he gives it a peculiar sense. He eliminates the problem for himself by assuming that the entities that are phenomenally given *are* the entities that are." [84]

It should not surprise us, in the light of what has thus far been said in this chapter, that Heidegger regards Nietzsche as a metaphysician. By transforming truth into a mode of the will-to-power, Nietzsche represents the culmination of the de-ontologized subjectivization of truth, for Heidegger. Heidegger deals with Nietzsche's concept of truth as an intensification of Descartes' thesis that truth resides in the understanding, and a culmination of Platonic *orthotes*.

And in the age in which the fulfillment of modern times commences Nietzsche sharpens the above statement ["truth or falsehood in the genuine sense cannot be anywhere else except in the understanding alone."] even more: *"Truth is the kind of error* without which a certain kind of living being could not live. The value for *life* decides in the end." (Notation made in 1885, *The Will to Power*, n. 493)). If truth according to Nietzsche is a kind of error, then its essence lies in the manner of thinking which always and necessarily falsifies the real, in so far as every act of representation causes the unexposed "becoming" to be still and sets up something that does not correspond (i.e. something incorrect) with what

[83] *Platons Lehre von der Wahrheit,* p. 5: "Die 'Lehre' eines Denkers ist das in seinem Sagen Ungesagte."
[84] *Truth and Art,* p. 157.

has thus been established in contradistinction to fluent "becoming;" thereby establishing something erroneous as the allegedly real. In Nietzsche's defining of truth as incorrectness of thinking, there lies the concession to thinking of the traditional essence of truth as the correctness of making an assertion (*logos*). Nietzsche's concept of truth is an example of the last reflection of the extreme consequences of that changing of truth from the unconcealment of beings to the correctness of the glance. The change itself takes place in the definition of the Being of beings (i.e., according to the Greeks, the presence of what is present) as *idea*.[85]

Heidegger's interest in Nietzsche as a "metaphysician," is intimately connected with Heidegger's thesis about the fate of truth and Being in the history of philosophy. Nietzsche's concept of truth as a certain kind of "error," brings the fulfillment of Heidegger's drama. The identification of "truth" and "error" suggests three things to Heidegger. (1) Nietzsche's concept of truth is "an example of the last reflection of the extreme consequences" which the transformation from *alétheia* to *orthotes* inevitably occasions. It represents the dis-essence of *orthotes*; the inversion of Platonic truth. (2) The identification of "truth" and "error" is nonetheless epistemological in character, hence, "humanistic" and subjectivistic. (3) The "extreme consequences" implicit in Plato's humanistic-epistemological concept of truth become fully explicit in Nietzsche, through the identification of the Being of beings with "will." Truth devolves historically from *alétheia* (pre-Platonic), to *orthotes* (Plato), to *adequatio intellectus et rei* (medieval), to certitude (Descartes), to error (Nietzsche). As a consequence of the devolution of truth, Being devolves from *Anwesenheit* (pre-

---

[85] *Platons Lehre von der Wahrheit*, pp. 45–46: "Und im Zeitalter der anhebenden Vollendung der Neuzeit sagt Nietzsche in einer nochmaligen Verschärfung des vorigen Satzes: "*Wahrheit ist die Art von Irrtum,* ohne welche eine bestimmte Art von lebendigen Wesen nicht leben könnte. Der Wert für *das Leben* entscheidet zuletzt.' (Aufzeichnung aus dem Jahr 1885, Der Wille zur Macht, n. 493) Wenn die Wahrheit nach Nietzsche eine Art von Irrtum ist, dann liegt ihr Wesen in einer Weise des Denkens, die das Wirkliche jedesmal und zwar notwendig verfälscht, insofern nämlich jedes Vorstellen das unausgesetzte 'Werden' still stellt und mit dem so Festgestellten gegenüber fliessenden 'Werden' ein Nichtentsprechendes, d.h. Unrichtiges und somit ein Irriges als das angebliche Wirkliche aufstellt.

"In Nietzsche's Bestimmung der Wahrheit als der Unrichtigkeit des Denkens liegt die Zustimmung zum überlieferten Wesen der Wahrheit als der Richtigkeit des Aussagens (*logos*). Nietzsches Begriff der Wahrheit zeigt den letzten Wiederschein der äussersten Folge jenes Wandels der Wahrheit aus der Unverborgenheit des Seienden zur Richtigkeit des Blickens. Der Wandel selbst vollzieht sich in der Bestimmung des Sein des Seienden (d.h. griechisch der Anwesung des Anwesenden) als *idea*."

Platonic "presence" of what is unconcealed), to *Idea* (Plato), to *tran-scendens* (medieval period), to "will" (modern period).

The term "will" is central not only to Nietzsche, Heidegger main-tains, but represents the *essential* determination of Being after Des-cartes:

. . . let us observe the essential character in which the being of beings ap-pears within modern metaphysics. That essential character of Being finds its classic expression in a few sentences written by Schelling in 1809, in his *Philosophical Investigation Concerning the Nature of Human Freedom and its Object.* They declare "In the final and highest instance there is no being other than willing. Willing is primal being and to it alone (willing) belong all (primal being's) predicates; being unconditioned, eternity, in-dependence of time, self-affirmation. All philosophy strives only to find this highest expression." (F. W. J. Schelling, vol. 1, p. 419).

Schelling finds the predicates which thought has since antiquity attrib-uted to Being, in their final, highest and hence most perfected form in willing. But, the will in this willing does not here denote a capacity of the human soul. The word "willing" here signifies the Being of beings as a whole. It is will. That sounds strange to us, and indeed is strange as long as we remain strangers to the sustaining thoughts of Western metaphysics. And we will remain strangers as long as we do not think these thoughts but merely go on forever reporting them. We can, for instance, ascertain Leibniz's assertions about the Being of beings, with historical precision, and yet never think a jot of what he thought when he defined the Being of beings from the perspective of the monad, as the unity of *perceptio* and *appetitus,* the unity of representation and striving, that is as will. The object of Leibniz's thought finds expression through Kant and Fichte as the rational will which Hegel and Schelling, each in his own way, then reflects upon. Schopenhauer has the same thing in mind when he titles his major work *The World* (not Man) *as Will and Representation.* And Nietzsche thinks the same thing when he recognizes the primal being of beings as the will to power.[86]

[86] *Vorträge und Aufsätze* (Neske, 1959), pp. 113–114: ". . . achten wir darauf, in welcher Wesensprägung das Sein des Seienden innerhalb der neuzeitlichen Metaphysik erscheint. Diese Wesensprägung des Seins kommt in einer klas-sischen Form durch wenige Sätze zur Sprache, die Schelling in seinen 'Philo-sophischen Untersuchungen über das Wesen der menschlichen Freiheit und die damit zusammenhängende Gegenstände' 1809 niedergelegt hat. Die drei Sätze lauten: '– Es gibt in der letzten und höchsten Instanz gar kein andres Seyn als Wollen. Wollen ist Urseyn und auf dieses (das Wollen) allein passen alle Prädi-kate desselben (des Urseyns): Grundlosigkeit, Ewigkeit, Unabhängigkeit von der Zeit, Selbstbejahung. Die ganze Philosophie strebt nur dahin, diesen höchsten Ausdruck zu finden" (F. W. Schellings philosophische Schriften, 1 Bd., Landshut 1809, S. 419).

"Schelling findet die Prädikate, die das Denken der Metaphysik von altersher dem Sein zuspricht, nach ihrer letzten und höchsten und somit vollendeten Ge-

In the above quotation, Heidegger identifies "modern metaphysics" with the German tradition. Within it, from Leibniz to Nietzsche, the Being of beings allegedly appears as will. It should be noted, then, that Heidegger works out of two, not one, set of preconceptions. When he analyzes the writings of a specific philosopher, his interpretation emerges from the context of the question of Being. He is, admittedly, more concerned about what happens to Being and truth in Plato, for example, then with what Plato had to say explicitly about either one. However questionable this procedure may be from the standpoint of an historian of philosophy, with his emphasis upon textual fidelity, excessive irritation misses the point. Heidegger is not writing a history of philosophy. He is writing a metahistory; a philosophy *of* the history of philosophy – however the fruits of his labors are to be evaluated. However, it is one thing to write a history of philosophy which is guided by the question of Being, but quite another thing to write a partial history. And the Being-question involves us in a terribly selective view of the tradition. Why is "modern metaphysics" the movement of German philosophy? If the Being-question commits us to stating what a specific thinker did *not* say, as Heidegger's method announces, does it also commit us to ignoring what others *have* said? Spinoza, Locke, Berkeley, and Hume are ignored, by Heidegger, within "modern metaphysics." On what grounds are they ignored? Does Being appear as will in each? If so, why ignore them? If not, what is the meaning of the claim that the Being of beings appears within modern metaphysics as will? To these questions Heidegger gives no hint of an answer.

Heidegger's philosophy of Western metaphysics involves two internally connected matrices. The first matrix, from Plato to Descartes,

---

stalt im Wollen. Der Wille dieses Wollens ist hier jedoch nicht als Vermögen der menschlichen Seele gemeint. Das Wort 'Wollen' nennt hier das Sein des Seienden im Ganzen. Dieses ist Wille. Das klingt uns befremdlich und ist es auch, solange uns die tragenden Gedanken der abendländischen Metaphysik fremd bleiben. Dies bleiben sie, solange wir diese Gedanken nicht denken, sondern nur immer über sie berichten. Man kann z.B. die Aussagen von Leibniz über das Sein des Seienden von der Monade aus als die Einheit von perceptio und appetitus, als Einheit von Vorstellen und Anstreben, d.h. als Wille bestimmte. Was Leibniz denkt, kommt durch Kant und Fichte als der Vernunftwille zur Sprache, dem Hegel und Schelling, jeder auf seine Weise, nachdenken. Das Selbe meint Schopenhauer, wenn er seinem Hauptwerk den Titel gibt: 'Die Welt (nicht der Mensch) als Wille und Vorstellung.' Das Selbe denkt Nietzsche, wenn er das Ursein des Seienden als Wille zur Macht erkennt."

involves the de-volution of truth from non-concealment to certitude. The second matrix consists of the *consequent* interpretation of Being as will.

With the final triumph of certitude over *alétheia* – in Descartes – the correspondence between idea and representation proceeds from the "idea," as the ontologically prior datum to which the representation must conform. The epistemological (correspondence) criterion of truth can begin with either element in the polarity – idea or representation.[87] In Plato and Aristotle, for example, the proposition was "true" if it expressed the ontologically prior and independently real "thing" (whether Form, primary or secondary substance) to which it referred. In Descartes, for Heidegger, beings *are* only if they approximate the subjective self-certainty of the subject. That is, beings *are* by conforming to the ontologically prior standard of truth as certitude. It is this phenomenon that Heidegger views as the beginning of the interpretation of Being as will. In so far as beings *are,* to the extent that they conform to the criterion of the human subject, it is man who bestows "existence" upon beings. The Being of beings coincides with man's positing of existence. Beings are revealed in their truth, i.e., beings *are,* because their existence cannot be doubted by the knowing subject.

It should be stressed, in concluding this chapter, that Heidegger does not regard the emphasis upon will as a development peculiar to German idealism. For Heidegger, post-Kantian idealism is but a stark expression of the "voluntarism"[88] of the entire post-Cartesian period.

[87] Although the suggestion that the representation must conform to the idea might more nearly approximate the coherence theory of truth, Heidegger makes no such distinction. Nor does he interpret the conformity of "thing" to "idea" as a distinct sense of truth, as was pointed out in our discussion of Hofstadter's "truth of things" above. At issue for Heidegger is not the question of what conforms to what, but the fact that the criterion *is* a relationship of conformity as such. When truth consists of the "object's" conformity to the "subject," Being is conceived as will.

[88] The term "voluntarism" is here to be understood in Heidegger's sense, as the determination of the Being of beings as will.

CHAPTER II

NIETZSCHE AS METAPHYSICIAN

The broad outlines of Heidegger's interpretation of Nietzsche first appeared in an essay entitled "Nietzsche's Phrase 'God is Dead.'"[1] It consists of a highly compressed summary of Heidegger's reflections on Nietzsche covering the period 1936–1940. The lecture material on which that essay is based was later published in two volumes.[2]

The essay correctly takes Nietzsche's assertions about God to refer not only to the God of Christianity, but to any absolute whatsoever. The "death" of God signifies the death of the suprasensible realm as such. It is the death of the timeless and eternal as the ground and meaning of the temporal. It expresses the death of the "true world."[3] If a dichotomy is to be drawn between the apparent and the real, the transitory and the eternal, the contingent and the necessary, then the death of God proclaims the demise of the real, eternal, and necessary. In so far as the polarity between the apparent and the real, becoming and being, is essentially a Platonic polarity, Heidegger takes Nietzsche's word "God" to refer to the transempirical, i.e., *metaphysical* realm. For Heidegger, Nietzsche's "God" symbolizes the order of metaphysics.

> God is the name for the domain of ideas and ideals. This domain of the suprasensible has been considered since Plato, more precisely since the late Greek and Christian interpretation of the Platonic philosophy, as the true and actually real world . . . The phrase "God is dead" means: the suprasensible world is without active power. It emits no life. Metaphysics, i.e. for Nietzsche Western philosophy conceived as Platonism, is at an end.[4]

---

[1] *Holzwege* (Frankfurt a/Main: Klostermann, 1950), pp. 193–247.

[2] *Nietzsche,* I and II (Pfullingen: Neske, 1961).

[3] Cf. GOA VIII, *Die Götzendämmerung,* 82.

[4] *Holzwege,* (Frankfurt a/Main: Klostermann, 1950), pp. 199–200: "Gott ist der Name für den Bereich der Ideen und der Ideale. Dieser Bereich des Über-

... In the phrase "God is dead" the name God, thought through essentially, stands for the suprasensible world of ideals which contains the enduring goal beyond earthly life for this life and defines it in this manner from above and so, in a certain sense, from outside.[5]

To assert the "death" of God is to proclaim the death of the metaphysical realm, in the sense that the metaphysical has lost its power as a viable determiner of the phenomenal realm, has failed to give direction to the human condition, has left Being valueless. This loss of meaning is experienced and characterized by Nietzsche as the emergence of nihilism. "What does nihilism mean? ... *That the highest values become devalued.*"[6] The "death of God" proclaims the age of nihilism, the triumph of nothing, to which Nietzsche stands witness. Heidegger, of course, is persuaded that this nihilism is already molded in Plato's doctrine of truth, and that its expression coincides with the history of metaphysics. "In its essence, however, metaphysics is nihilism."[7] Heidegger equates nihilism with the forgetfulness of Being. Since "metaphysics," in Heidegger's sense, has been characterized by the triumph of epistemological truth over ontological truth, Being is "conceptualized" in metaphysics through the tacit assumption of the criteria of universality, undefinability and self-evidence. In consequence, for Heidegger, nihilism begins with Plato since he affected the first radical transformation of *alétheia*. Moreover, Heidegger generally assumes that nihilism designates the same historical movement for Nietzsche. This is not at all obvious. Although there is some evidence to support this view (*viz.*, Nietzsche's conception of metaphysics as "fable" and "error,"[8] and philosophy as an expression of the will-to- power), Nietzsche's attitude toward Western philosophy is more ambivalent than Heidegger acknowl-

---

sinnlichen gilt seit Platon, genauer gesagt, seit der spätgriechischen und christlichen Auslegung der Platonischen Philosophie, als die wahre und eigentlich wirkliche Welt ... Das Wort 'Gott is tot' bedeutet: die übersinnliche Welt ist ohne wirkende Kraft. Sie spendet kein Leben. Die Metaphysik, d.h. für Nietzsche die abendländische Philosophie als Platonismus verstanden, ist zu Ende."

[5] *Ibid.*, p. 203: "In dem Wort 'Gott ist tot' steht der Name Gott, wesentlich gedacht, für die übersinnliche Welt der Ideale, die das über dem irdischen Leben bestehende Ziel für dieses Leben enthalten und es dergestalt von oben und so in gewisser Weise von aussen her bestimmen."

[6] GOA *Nachlass* XVI 2: "Was bedeutet Nihilismus? ... *Dass die obersten Werte sich entwerten.*"

[7] *Nietzsche,* vol. I, p. 245: "In ihrem Wesen aber ist die Metaphysik Nihilismus ..."

[8] Cf. Chapter III, Part I.

edges. On the one hand, Nietzsche despairs of the possibility of "truth" in any quasi-objective sense.[9] Although Heidegger is correct in insisting that "knowledge . . . is, in essence, the schematization of a Chaos"[10] for Nietzsche, Nietzsche nevertheless regarded this "error" as historically necessary and fruitful. In short, when Nietzsche refers to "nihilism" he generally refers to the *destruction* of the "real" world. That is not to suggest that Nietzsche deems a return to an all-embracing system either as possible or desirable. For that too would be an error. But as a *necessary* illusion, the disappearance of "truth," system, leaves man aimless, groundless; floundering in a becoming without direction or purpose: *"With the true world we have abolished the apparent one as well."*[11]

This difference in Heidegger's and Nietzsche's conception of nihilism is not only philosophically interesting, but offers us perhaps the best brief example of Heidegger's interpretive methodology at work. He begins by acknowledging Nietzsche's conception of nihilism, then broadens its meaning through his own conception of nihilism and, finally, attributes his own conception as implicit in Nietzsche's. Distinctions finally collapse. After acknowledging that, for Nietzsche, the death of God signifies the devaluation of the highest values, hence the emergence of nihilism, Heidegger begins to reflect on the phenomenon of nihilism itself.

The domain of the essence and event of nihilism is metaphysics itself, always granting that with this term we do not designate a doctrine or even merely a special discipline of philosophy, but think of the basic relational pattern (*Grundgefüge*) of beings as a whole, in so far as it is distinguished into a sensible and suprasensible world and is sustained and defined by this distinction. Metaphysics is the historic sphere within which it becomes destiny that the suprasensible world, the ideas, God, the moral law, the authority of reason, progress, the happiness of the greatest number, culture, forfeit and annul their generative force in civilization. We call this essential deterioration of the suprasensible its "disessence" (*Verwesung*). Disbelief, in the sense of the apostasy of the Christian religious doctrine, is therefore never the essence and basis but rather only a consequence of

---

[9] Cf. *Will to Power,* 493: "Truth is the kind of error without which a certain kind of living being could not live."

[10] *Nietzsche,* vol. I, p. 559: "Erkennen . . . ist im Grunde das 'Schematisieren' eines Chaos."

[11] GOA VIII *Die Götzendämmerung,* 82: *"mit der wahren Welt haben wir auch die Scheinbare abgeschafft."*

nihilism; for it could be that Christianity itself represents a consequence and development of nihilism.[12]

This passage succinctly expresses Heidegger's conception of nihilism. The second sense in which Heidegger uses the term "metaphysics," discussed in the previous chapter, once again appears. Metaphysics is identified not with a philosophic discipline or doctrine, but with Western man's relationship to beings as such – "the basic relational pattern of beings as a whole." "Metaphysics" here signifies the historical mode of Western man's relationship to beings, implicitly the forgetfulness of Being–nihilism. The deterioration of the supra-sensible represents, for Heidegger, a disessence, a dissimulation, which marks a stage in the progress of the de-volution of Being – "the historic sphere within which it becomes destiny." But if the "death of God" is merely the fulfillment of metaphysics, which *is* the forgetfulness of Being, then it is a consequence of, rather than the cause of, nihilism. Heidegger assimilates the "death of God" as an event *within* nihilism rather than conceiving it as the *advent* of nihilism. Yet Nietzsche did not conceive the relationship in this way. The "death of God" is, for Nietzsche, the devaluation of the highest values, which he defines *as* nihilism: "What does nihilism mean? . . . *That the highest values become devalued.*"[13] As a consequence of this devaluation *"With the true world we have abolished the apparent one as well."*[14] Nihilism is the extreme consequence of the abolition of the "true world," not the event of positing the distinction between an apparent and true world. But Heidegger, concerned with finding his own analysis of nihilism already dormant in Nietzsche's, comes full circle and

---

[12] *Holzwege,* p. 204: "Der Bereich für das Wesen und das Ereignis des Nihilismus ist die Metaphysik selbst, immer gesetzt, dass wir bei diesem Namen nicht eine Lehre oder gar nur eine Soderdisziplin der Philosophie meinen, sondern an das Grundgefüge des Seienden im Ganzen denken, sofern dieses in eine sinnliche und übersinnliche Welt unterschieden und jene von dieser getragen und bestimmt wird. Die Metaphysik ist der Geschichtsraum, worin zum Geschick wird, dass die übersinnliche Welt, die Ideen, Gott, das Sittengesetz, die Vernunftautorität, der Fortschritt, das Glück der Meisten, die Kultur, die Zivilisation ihre bauende Kraft einbüssen und nichtig werden. Wir nennen diesen Wesenszerfall des Übersinnlichen seine Verwesung. Der Unglaube im Sinne des Abfalls von der Christlichen Glaubenslehre ist daher niemals das Wesen und der Grund, sondern stets nur eine Folge des Nihilismus; denn es könnte sein dass das Christentum selbst nur eine Folge und Ausformung des Nihilismus darstellt."

[13] GOA *Nachlass* XVI, 2.

[14] GOA VIII *Die Götzendämmerung,* 82.

ascribes to Nietzsche the view that nihilism is the "inner logic" of Western history. It is at this point that Heidegger superimposes *his* conception and grafts it on to Nietzsche's view of nihilism.

Only for Nietzsche nihilism is by no means merely an emergence of deterioration. Rather, nihilism is at the same time the basic process of Western history and, above all, the lawfulness of this history. That is also why, in his observations concerning nihilism, it matters less to Nietzsche to historically depict the termination of the process of devaluing of the highest values and to calculate the decline of the West from that; rather, Nietzsche conceives nihilism as the "inner logic" of Western history.[15]

It is true that nihilism, for *Heidegger,* represents the basic process of Western history, conceived as an "inner logic" of successive radicalizations of man's forgetfulness of Being, through the triumph of epistemological truth which, in turn, culminates in its own self-negation – truth as error. But it is extremely doubtful that Nietzsche conceived nihilism as either the "basic process" or "inner logic" of Western history. The "death of God" probably did not proclaim the "inner logic" of Western history, conceived as "metaphysics," for Nietzsche.

A more accurate account would acknowledge the interdependence of metaphysics *and* religion as the context within which Nietzsche's conception of nihilism emerges. In addition, Nietzsche had a reasonably recent historical period in mind when he referred to the advent of nihilism. "The greatest new event – that 'God is dead,' that belief in the Christian God has become unbelievable – already begins to cast its first shadows over Europe." [16] The death of God, as the apostasy of Christian doctrine – not only "metaphysics" – is a "new event." A "new event" is hardly the "basic process of Western

---

[15] *Holzwege,* p. 206: "Allein für Nietzsche ist der Nihilismus keineswegs nur eine Verfallserscheinung, sondern der Nihilismus ist als Grundvorgang der abendländischen Geschichte zugleich und vor allem die Gesetzlichkeit dieser Geschichte. Deshalb liegt Nietzsche auch bei seinen Betrachtungen über den Nihilismus weniger daran, den Ablauf des Vorganges der Entwertung der obersten Werte historisch zu schildern und schliesslich daraus den Untergang des Abendlandes zu errechnen, sondern Nietzsche denkt den Nihilismus als die 'innere Logik' der abendländischen Geschichte."

[16] *Werke in Drei Bänden, Fröhliche Wissenschaft,* p. 205: "Das grösste neuere Ereignis – dass 'Gott tot ist,' dass der Glaube an den christlichen Gott unglaubwürdig geworden ist – beginnt bereits seine ersten Schatten über Europa zu werfen."

history." A more accurate assessment by far, of Nietzsche's concept of nihilism, is to be found in the work of Arthur Danto.

Professor Danto takes Nietzsche's doctrine to be a nihilism distinguishable from the incomplete "nihilism, which flourished in the latter decades of the nineteenth century in Europe, especially in the 1850's and 1860's in Russia . . ." [17] The nihilism of the nineteenth century, to which Nietzsche responded, reacted "as though the needs and hopes which had found satisfaction in religion still perdured in an era when religion itself no longer could be credited, and something else – sciences, education, revolution, evolution, socialism, business enterprise, or, latterly, sex – must be seized upon to fill the place left empty and to discharge the office vacated by religious beliefs which could not now sustain." [18] Nietzsche's own nihilism, which he sometimes characterized as a pessimism beyond good and evil, thus became the foundation for his critique of philosophy and nineteenth century nihilism as well.

Nietzsche's critique of other philosophies rests upon a psychological thesis that each metaphysical system ever advanced was due, in the end, to a need to find order and security in the world, a position where the mind might "repose and recreate itself." Each system provided, accordingly, a consolatory account of things in which this might be possible. Nietzsche was persuaded that all such views were false. The problem then was to exhibit their invalidity, determine why people should have thought them viable, and then go on living in the full recognition of the inviability of every possible religious and metaphysical assurance. [19]

In response to the unreflective nihilism of his contemporaries, Nietzsche advanced his own.

. . . by "Nihilism" he had in mind a thoroughly disillusioned conception of a world which is as hostile to human aspirations as he could imagine it to be. It is hostile not because it, or anything other than us, has goals of its own, but because it is utterly indifferent to what we either believe or hope . . . To be able to accept and affirm such a view he thought required considerable courage, for it meant that we must abandon hopes and expectations which had comforted men, through religions and philosophies, from the beginning. For the attitude he felt he could and we should adopt, he provided the formula of *Amor Fati* – loving one's fate, accepting, without palliative or protection, the results of a most thorough-going critique of the philosophical and scientific ideas, seen as fictions, the

[17] *Nietzsche as Philosopher* (New York: Macmillan, 1965), p. 29.
[18] *Ibid.*, pp. 29–30.
[19] *Ibid.*, pp. 34–35.

products of some human need for security; and then endeavoring to live in a world impervious to these needs, to say Yes to the cosmic insignificance, not only of oneself and of human beings generally but also of life and nature as a whole.[20]

Heidegger and Nietzsche both respond to a phenomenon of nihilism. However, whereas Heidegger locates the origin of the phenomenon in Plato and regards it as synonymous with "metaphysics" itself, Nietzsche generally considers nihilism as a later outgrowth of the dissolution of post-Platonic metaphysics and, above all, of religious belief. Heidegger ignores such distinctions in his treatment of Nietzsche and is, at best, only partially correct in finding confirmation of his own diagnosis in Nietzsche's thinking.

One of Nietzsche's central tasks was the confrontation with nihilism, involving the transvaluation of traditional values which had left Being valueless. The transvaluation does not merely involve the substitution of one set of values for an older, corroded, set of values. An effective transvaluation must reverse, or call into question, the foundations upon which the value positing activity rests. Nietzsche believed that this could be accomplished by affirming precisely what he thought the Western tradition had suppressed after Heraclitus: becoming.

In this sense I have the right to regard myself as the first *tragic philosopher* – that is, the extreme antithesis and antipode of a pessimistic philosopher. Before me the transformation of the dionysian into a philosophic pathos does not exist: *tragic wisdom* is lacking – I have sought in vain for signs of it even among the *great* philosophers, those belonging to the two centuries before Socrates. I still retained a doubt about *Heraclitus*, in whose company I feel better, more cheerful than anywhere else. Saying Yes to the flux *and destruction,* the decisive element in a dionysian philosophy, saying Yes to contradiction and strife, to *becoming,* together with the radical rejection of even the concept *"Being"* – in this I must, in any case, acknowledge that which has the closest affinity to my thought hitherto.[21]

---

[20] *Ibid.,* pp. 33–34.

[21] GOA XV, *Ecce Homo,* 65: "In diesem Sinne habe ich das Recht, mich selber als den ersten *tragischen Philosophen* zu verstehen – dass heisst den äussersten Gegensatz und Antipoden eines pessimistischen Philosophen. Vor mir gibt es diese Umsetzung des dionysischen in ein philosophisches Pathos nicht: es fehlt die *tragische Weisheit* – ich habe vergebens nach Anzeichen davon selbst bei den *grossen* Griechen der Philosophie, denen der zwei Jahrhunderte *vor* Sokrates, gesucht. Ein Zweifel blieb mir zurück bei *Heraklit,* in dessen Nähe überhaupt mir wärmer, mir wohler zumute wird als irgendwo sonst. Die Be-

Nietzsche affirms becoming, according to Heidegger, not as a mute and aimless procession, but as the will-to-power which concretizes itself as eternal recurrence of the same. For Heidegger, will-to-power and eternal recurrence are two aspects of a single phenomenon (not unlike Spinoza's *natura naturans* and *natura naturata*). Nietzsche conceives of "Being i.e., the will-to-power, *as* eternal recurrence";[22] "However, the will-to-power *is* as eternal recurrence."[23] "Will-to-power" and "eternal recurrence" are both referred to, by Heidegger, as the Being of beings. They are two expressions of Being: "The two fundamental terms of Nietzsche's metaphysics, 'will-to-power' and 'eternal recurrence of the same,' determine beings in their Being in those aspects which have guided metaphysics since antiquity, *ens qua ens* in the sense of *essentia* and *existentia*."[24]

Although we are principally concerned with the doctrine of eternal recurrence, its aspect as will-to-power must be briefly examined – since Heidegger conceives them to be inseparable. "In Nietzsche's language, will-to-power, becoming, life, and Being, mean, in the broadest sense, the same thing."[25]

"Will-to-power" and "eternal recurrence" constitute the new becoming, the transvaluation of nihilism.

The bare and undefined word "becoming" does not here mean, nor generally in the conceptual language of Nietzsche's metaphysics, one or another flux of all things; not the bare change of states, nor even one or another development and undetermined unfolding. "Becoming" means the transition from something to something; that movement and agitation which Leibniz, in the *Monadology* (# 11), calls the "changements

---

jahung des Vergehens *und Vernichtens,* das Entscheidende in einer dionysischen Philosophie, das Jasagen zu Gegensatz und Krieg, das *Werden,* mit radikaler Ablehnung auch selbst des Begriffs 'Sein' – darin muss ich unter allen Umständen das mir Verwandteste anerkennen, was bisher gedacht worden ist."

[22] *Nietzsche,* vol. I (Pfullingen: Neske, 1961), p. 28: "Nietzsche denkt und betrachtet . . . das Sein, d.h. den Willen zur Macht, als ewige Wiederkehr."

[23] *Ibid.,* p. 160: "Der Wille zur Macht aber *ist* als die ewige Wiederkehr."

[24] *Holzwege,* (Frankfurt a/Main: Klostermann, 1952), p. 219: ". . . Die beiden Grundworte der Metaphysik Nietzsches, 'Wille zur Macht' und 'ewige Wiederkunft des Gleichen,' bestimmen das Seiende in seinem Sein nach den Hinsichten, die von altersher für die Metaphysik leitend bleiben, das ens qua ens im Sinne von essentia und existentia." Cf. also *Nietzsche,* vol. I, pp. 425, 464–467; *Nietzsche,* vol. II, pp. 283–287.

[25] *Ibid.,* p. 213: "Wille zur Macht, Werden, Leben und Sein im weitesten Sinne bedeuten in Nietzsches Sprache das Selbe." Cf. also *Vorträge und Aufsätze,* pp. 103, 115; *Nietzsche,* vol. I, pp. 44–46.

naturels" which pervade the *ens qua ens,* i.e., the *ens percipiens et appetens.* Nietzsche thinks this governing force as the fundamental feature of everything real, i.e., in a broader sense beings. He grasps that which determines beings in their *essentia* as the "will-to-power" . . . "Becoming" is, for Nietzsche, the "will-to-power." The "will-to-power" is thus the fundamental feature of "life," which word Nietzsche often employs with the broad meaning according to which it has been identified with "becoming" within metaphysics (compare Hegel). In Nietzsche's language, will-to-power, becoming, life and Being, mean, in the broadest sense, the same thing.[26]

As has been stated in the preceding chapter, Heidegger conceives the essential determination of Being, within modern (post-Cartesian) subjectivism, voluntaristically i.e., as will. In consequence the "will" is neither a psychological nor a biological (Darwinian) category. "Willing is to will mastery."[27] But the will to mastery is not to be understood as the expression of power as an urge for domination. Rather "Every willing is a willing-to-be-more. Power only exists in so far and to the extent that it remains a willing-to-be-more-power."[28] The will-to-power, as Heidegger interprets it, is essentially a will to self-affirmation, strengthening and increasing one's being. Far from being a psychological reality, this is an ontological state common to all beings: "The will wills itself."[29] The difficulty involved in conceiving the will-to-power ontologically is, for Heidegger, neither more nor less difficult than properly understanding the appearance of Being as will in post-Cartesian thought. "That the Being of beings here

---

[26] *Ibid.,* pp. 212–213: "Das blosse und unbestimmte Wort Werden bedeutet hier und überhaupt in der Begriffssprache der Metaphysik Nietzsches nicht irgendein Fliessen aller Dinge, nicht den blossen Wechsel der Zustände, auch nicht irgendeine Entwicklung und unbestimmte Entfaltung. 'Werden' meint den Übergang von etwas zu etwas, jene Bewegung und Bewegtheit, die Leibniz in der Monadologie (# 11) die changements naturels nennt, die das en qua ens, d.h. das ens percipiens et appetens durchwaltet. Nietzsche denkt dieses Waltende als den Grundzug alles Wirklichen, d.h. im weiteren Sinne Seienden. Er begreift das, was so das Seiende in essentia bestimmt als den 'Willen zur Macht.' . . . 'Das Werden,' das ist für Nietzsche 'Der Wille zur Macht.' Der 'Wille zur Macht' ist so der Grundzug des 'Lebens,' welches Wort Nietzsche oft auch in der weiten Bedeutung gebraucht, nach der es innerhalb der Metaphysik (vgl. Hegel) mit 'Werden' gleichgesetzt worden ist. Wille zur Macht, Werden, Leben und Sein im weitesten Sinne bedeuten in Nietzsches Sprache das Selbe."

[27] *Ibid.,* p. 216: "Wollen ist Herr-sein-wollen." Cf. also, *Nietzsche,* vol. I, pp. 50–52.

[28] *Nietzsche,* vol. I, p. 72: "Jedes Wollen ist ein Mehr-sein-wollen. Macht selbst ist nur, sofern und solange sie ein Mehr-Macht-sein-wollen bleibt."

[29] *Ibid.,* p. 216: "Der Wille will sich selbst."

emerges throughout as will, does not depend upon opinions a few philosophers have formed about beings. What this appearance of Being as will signifies, no learned analysis will ever disclose." [30] Setting aside the pronouncement that no learned analysis will ever disclose what Being as will signifies, it is sufficient for our purposes to recognize that by conceiving Being as will-to-power, Nietzsche identifies it as the fundamental basis which beings themselves *are*. It is the fundamental feature of beings, whose reality consists of growth, heightening, intensification, and self-mastery. Being, conceived as will, is self-moving, self-willing. For Heidegger, Nietzsche's conception of willing as the indwelling structure of beings comes closer to the pre-Platonic sense of *physis* than any notion in the subsequent history of metaphysics.

In order to avoid unnecessary misunderstandings, Heidegger points out that "will-to-power," as the Being of beings, is not to be conceived as a substance underlying beings. The traditional dichotomy of substance and attribute, essence and existence, real and apparent, is not repeated in the relationship between beings and will-to-power.

The essential unity of the will-to-power can be no other than itself. It is the mode in which the will-to-power thrusts itself, as will, before itself. It [will-to-power] posits itself [will] before itself in its own ordeal [*Prüfung*] in such a manner that, in such an ordeal, it represents itself as pure, and thus represents itself in its highest form. But the representation is here by no means a subsequent presentation, rather, the presence determined by it [will-to-power] is the mode in which and as which the will-to-power *is*.[31]

Stripped of some of its more obscure overtones, Martin Heidegger's point agrees remarkably with Arthur Danto's later independent treatment of the same subject.

---

[30] *Vorträge und Aufsätze* (Pfullingen: Neske, 1954), p. 114: "Dass hier überall das Sein des Seienden durchgängig als Wille erscheint, beruht nicht auf Ansichten, die sich einige Philosophen über das Seiende zurechtlegen. Was dieses Erscheinen des Seins als Wille heisst, wird keine Gelehrsamkeit je ausfindig machen . . ."

[31] *Holzwege*, p. 224: "Die Wesenseinheit des Willens zur Macht kann nichts anderes sein als er selbst. Sie ist die Weise, wie der Wille zur Macht als Wille sich vor sich selbst bringt. Sie stellt ihn selbst in seine eigene Prüfung und vor sie dergestalt, dass er in solcher Prüfung sich selbst erst rein und damit in seiner höchsten gestallt repräsentiert. Aber die Repräsentation ist hier keineswegs eine nachträgliche Darstellung, sondern die aus ihr bestimmte Präsenz ist die Weise, in welcher und als welche der Wille zur Macht *ist*."

It is hardly avoidable that we think of Will-to-Power in almost exactly the terms in which men once thought of substance, as that which underlies everything else and was the most fundamental of all. For Will-to-Power is not something we *have,* but something we *are.* Not only are *we* Will-to-Power, but so is everything, human and animal, animate and material. The entire world is Will-to-Power; there is nothing more basic, for there is nothing other than it and its modifications.

Plainly, then, Will-to-Power is an elemental concept in Nietzsche's thinking, a concept in whose terms everything is to be understood and to which everything is finally to be reduced. It is a metaphysical or, better, an ontological concept . . .[32]

Arthur Danto's interesting treatment agrees with Martin Heidegger's evaluation of the will-to-power concept in several important respects. Both treat the concept as ontological, as a designation of what exists. Moreover, both agree that everything is to be explained in terms of the will-to-power: "Nietzsche understands art, the state, religion, science, society, in terms of it."[33] Thus both agree that the concept is not only psychological. As Danto puts it: "But his notion of *will* is not purely psychological; the psychological volition, if we suppose it to be real, must be explained in terms of it."[34] "Will-to-Power" pervades and defines everything: "Because life is 'Will-to-Power,' concepts and values are expressions of the will and means for the exercise of will upon will. A living organism is apparently a collection of point-forces, operating in unison; the mental processes of higher organisms are but elaborations of dynamism lower down which are primordial prototypes of valuing and thinking. Degrees of complexity aside, the *function* remains the same throughout."[35] As was pointed out earlier, Heidegger and Danto also agree that the will to power constitutes an essential unity which has no existence apart from its concrete expression:

We are not to think in terms of "things" any longer, but in terms of dynamic quanta. Nietzsche has an argument in the *Nachlass* that a thing is simply the sum of "its" effects, so that if we eliminate the effects, hoping to isolate the thing as it "really" is, we will have nothing left. There is, as it were, no isolated thing which can be thought of on its own; there is only a community of effects, and, accordingly, the *Ding an sich* is an

---

[32] Arthur Danto, *Nietzsche as Philosopher,* p. 215.

[33] *Holzwege,* p. 213: "Als solche versteht Nietzsche die Kunst, den Staat, die Religion, die Wissenschaft, die Gesellschaft."

[34] *Nietzsche as Philosopher,* p. 217.

[35] *Ibid.,* p. 223.

empty word. This gives us a world of effects, but not effects *of* anything. And effects are not entities, detachable, as it were, to be studied on their own. If we regard effects as connected with Will-to-Power, we could regard them as effects of Will-to-Power, but Will-to-Power would not be an entity separate from them; they would *be* Will-to-Power. An effect might be regarded as the impact of will upon will, not the shock of thing upon thing. We might find it hard to grasp this idea . . .[36]

Heidegger's treatment of the unity of will-to-power agrees in its essential features with the above passage. Heidegger, in consequence, treats the will-to-power as a will to mastery, not in the sense of a psychological will to dominate and control, but as a "willing-to-be-more": "Every willing is a willing-to-be-more. Power itself only exists in so far and to the extent that it remains a willing-to-be-more-power."[37] Thus, this willing-to-be-more is a willing in which and as which "The will wills itself."[38] Arthur Danto states this will's self-willing in an equally striking way:

A force will tend to move outward forever until some external force impedes its dilation . . . Were it not resisted, a body (force) would occupy the whole of space. But there are other forces, each endeavoring to do the same. Each force occupies a territory (an area of space) and is pretty much what it is as the result of counterforces meeting and opposing its territorial expansion. We now might identify these outward forces as power centers (*Krafzentrum*), as Nietzsche sometimes calls them, or *will points* (*Willens-Punktationen*), "which continually either increase their power or lose it."[39]

For Heidegger, unlike Danto, we are involved in a two-fold unity. On the one hand, will-to-power and "its" particular expression are one. But, on the other hand, will-to-power and eternal recurrence are also one. "The two fundamental terms of Nietzsche's metaphysics, 'will to power' and 'eternal recurrence of the same,' determine beings in their Being in those aspects which have guided metaphysics since antiquity, *ens qua ens* in the sense of *essentia* and *existentia*."[40]

How then does this will find expression? How does it manifest itself as eternal recurrence of the same?

[36] *Ibid.,* pp. 219–220.

[37] *Nietzsche,* Vol. I, p. 72: "Jedes Wollen ist Mehr-sein-wollen. Macht selbst ist nur, sofern und so lange sie ein Mehr-Macht-sein-wollen bleibt."

[38] *Ibid.,* p. 216: "Der Wille will sich selbst."

[39] *Nietzsche as Philosopher,* p. 220.

[40] *Holzwege,* p. 219: "Die beiden Grundworte der Metaphysik Nietzsches, 'Wille zur Macht' und 'ewige Wiederkehr des Gleichen,' bestimmen das Seiende in seinem Sein nach den Hinsichten, die von altersher für die Metaphysik leitend bleiben, das ens qua ens im Sinne von essentia und existentia."

Of all of Heidegger's Nietzsche studies, the essay "Who is Nietzsche's Zarathustra?"[41] is perhaps the most impressive and illuminat-
ing. It lacks the repetitiousness of the two volumes of lecture material, as well as the fragmentary appearance of the essay in *Holzwege*.
Stylistically, it ranks among Heidegger's more poetic historical
studies. And in its treatment of "revenge" it adds valuable informa-
tion about Heidegger's understanding of the doctrine of eternal recurrence.

In this essay Zarathustra is interpreted as an "advocate" and "convalescent." He is an advocate in a three-fold sense. He speaks for the
benefit of something and for its justification. But in another and older
sense of "advocate," he fore-tells the advent of eternal recurrence. He
is an advocate, *Fuersprecher,* in the sense of a *Vor-sprecher,* some-
one who speaks in advance of something – a fore-shadower. This
advocacy is a kind of convalescence, for Heidegger: "The convalescent is the man who collects himself to return home, that is to turn in,
into his own destiny. The convalescent is on the road to himself, so
that he can say of himself who he is."[42] Zarathustra's extraordinary
advocacy constitutes the foreshadowing of his destiny; a destiny which
will heal the convalescent by enabling him to become who he is:
"I, Zarathustra, the advocate of life, the advocate of suffering, the
advocate of the circle . . ."[43] Heidegger cites this quotation to support
the position that the will-to-power ("life") and the eternal recurrence
("the circle") are related conceptions. Heidegger then moves one step
further and transforms the relationship into an identity: "These three
things, 'life, suffering, circle,' belong together, are the same."[44]
"Zarathustra presents himself as the advocate of the fact that all
being is will-to-power, which suffers as creative, colliding will and
thus wills itself in the eternal recurrence of the same."[45] The remainder of the essay is a suggestive attempt to deepen the meaning

[41] *Vorträge und Aufsätze,* pp. 101–126.

[42] *Ibid.,* p. 102: "Der Genesende ist derjenige, der sich zur Heimkehr sam-
melt, nämlich zur Einkehr in seine Bestimmung. Der Genesende ist unterwegs
zu ihm selber, so dass er von sich sagen kann, wer er ist."

[43] *Ibid.,* p. 102: "Ich, Zarathustra, der Fürsprecher des Lebens, der Fürsprecher des Leidens, der Fürsprecher des Kreises . . ."

[44] *Ibid.,* p. 102: "Diese Drei: 'Leben – Leiden – Kreis' gehören zusammen,
sind das Selbe."

[45] *Ibid.,* p. 103: "Demnach stellt sich Zarathustra als der Fürsprecher, dessen
vor, dass alles Seiende Wille zur Macht ist, der als schaffender, sich stossender
Wille leidet und so sich selber in der ewigen Wiederkehr des Gleichen will."

of this compressed statement. For, as this sentence stands in bare isolation, "We can write this definition down, memorize it, and produce it as needed . . ."[46] without reflecting on its meaning. In order to appropriate its meaning it is necessary to think it through, as Heidegger invariably tells his readers.

As the teacher of the overman and the eternal recurrence, Zarathustra – advocate and convalescent – "must first of all *become* who he is . . . 'behold, *you are the teacher of the eternal recurrence –* that is now *your* destiny!'"[47] In so far as Zarathustra is to become the teacher of eternal recurrence, "he obviously cannot begin with this doctrine."[48] Zarathustra teaches the doctrine of the overman as a prelude to eternal recurrence.

For Heidegger, the overman is necessary "Becaue Nietzsche recognizes the historical moment in which man prepares to assume dominion over the whole earth."[49] Hence, "the call of distress for the overman"[50] emerges from the question, "is man, as man in his nature till now prepared to assume dominion over the whole earth?"[51] Since man, in his past nature, has devalued the "apparent" and the "real" world, he must "be brought *beyond* himself . . ."[52] in order to assume dominion over the earth. Zarathustra is a bridge, according to Heidegger, from historical man to the overman, who alone can endure the thought of eternal recurrence, and assume dominion over the earth.

To fully comprehend the nature of the bridge, the transition from previous man and nihilism to the overman, three things must be observed, according to Heidegger; first, that from which the person crossing the bridge departs, second, the nature of the bridge itself and, third, the goal toward which we cross. And, as Heidegger reads Nietzsche, man (1) departs from the spirit of revenge, (2) across the

---

[46] *Ibid.,* "Wir können uns diese Definition aufschreiben, dem Gedächtnis einprägen und sie bei Gelegenheit nach Bedarf vorbringen."

[47] *Ibid.,* p. 105: "Zarathustra muss allererst derjenige *werden,* der er ist . . . 'siehe, du bist der Lehrer der ewigen Wiederkunft –, das ist nun *dein* Schicksal!'"

[48] *Ibid.,* ". . . kann er mit dieser Lehre auch nicht sogleich beginnen."

[49] *Ibid.,* p. 106: "Weil Nietzsche den geschichtlichen Augenblick erkennt, da der Mensch sich anschickt, die Herrschaft über die Erde im Ganzen anzutreten."

[50] *Ibid.,* ". . . der Notruf nach dem Übermenschen."

[51] *Ibid.,* "ist der Mensch als Mensch in seinem bisherigen Wesen für die Übernahme der Erdherrschaft vorbereitet?"

[52] *Ibid.,* "Muss dann der bisherige Mensch . . . über sich selbst hinaus gebracht werden."

[53] *Ibid.,* p. 120: "die heisst: Erlösung vom Geist der Rache."

bridge "which is called deliverance from the spirit of revenge," [53] (3) to the eternal recurrence of the same.

In "On the Tarantulas" Zarathustra says: "For *that man be delivered from revenge,* that is the bridge to the highest hope for me and a rainbow after long storms." [54] Heidegger observes that the nature of revenge, referred to here, is clearly delineated by Nietzsche in a subsequent section, "On Deliverance," in which Zarathustra says: "The spirit of revenge, my friends, has so far been the subject of man's best reflection." [55] Heidegger takes this sentence to mean: "This sentence relates revenge at the outset to all of mankind's reflections to this date." [56] By way of clarifying this interpretation, Heidegger goes on to say that "Here reflection means not just any pondering, but that thinking in which man's relation to what is, to all beings, is grounded and attuned . . . Nietzsche sees the nature and significance of revenge metaphysically." [57] In short, Heidegger suggests that revenge denotes, primarily, neither an ethical nor psychological category. "Revenge is here not a mere theme of morality nor is deliverance from revenge the task of moral education. Nor is revenge and vengefulness an object of psychology." [58] As in the case of the identification of Being and will, Heidegger broadens and deepens the meaning of "revenge." It designates the essence of Western thought.

As to the nature of revenge, the implicit force sustaining Western philosophy, Heidegger quotes the following Nietzsche sentence from "On Deliverance": "This, yes this alone, is *revenge* itself: the will's aversion to time and its 'It was.' " [59] Heidegger's interpretation of this sentence is typical. It is striking, apparently correct, and upon reflec-

[54] *Ibid.,* p. 110: "Denn *dass der Mensch erlöst werde von der Rache:* das ist mir die Brücke zur höchsten Hoffnung und ein Regenbogen nach langen Unwettern."

[55] *Ibid.,* p. 111: "*Der Geist der Rache:* Meine Freunde, das war bisher der Menschen bestes Nachdenken."

[56] *Ibid.,* p. 111: "Durch diesen Satz wird die Rache im vorhinein auf das ganze bisherige Nachdenken der Menschen bezogen."

[57] *Ibid.,* p. 111–112: "Das hier genannte Nachdenken meint nicht irgend ein Überlegen, sondern jenes Denken, worin das Verhältnis des Menschen zu dem beruht und schwingt, was ist, zum Seienden . . . Wesen und Tragweite der Rache sieht Nietzsche metaphysisch."

[58] *Ibid.,* p. 112: "Die Rache ist hier kein blosses Thema der Moral, und die Erlösung von der Rache keine Aufgabe der moralischen Erziehung. Ebensowenig bleibt die Rache und die Rachsucht ein Gegenstand der Psychologie."

[59] *Ibid.,* p. 115: "Dies, ja dies allein ist *Rache* selber: des Willens Widerwille gegen die Zeit und ihr 'Es war.' "

tion indistinguishable from Heidegger's own attitude and concern. It is, I believe, worth quoting at length:

Nietzsche defines revenge as "the will's aversion to time and its 'It was'." That appended definition ("It was") does not single out one characteristic of time by neglecting the other two. Rather, it identifies the foundation of time in its entire and intrinsic time-essence. Nietzsche's "and" in "time and its 'It was'," is not simply a transition to an additional specific feature of time. "And" here is the same thing as "and that means." Revenge is the will's aversion to time, and that means the ceasing to be and its transience. The will no longer has any influence over it, and its willing constantly runs up against it. Time and its "it was" is the stumbling-block which the will cannot budge. Time, as transience, is the adversity which the will suffers. As a suffering will, it suffers transience, wills its own cessation as suffering and, thereby, wills the disappearance of all things. The aversion to time degrades the transient. The earthly, the earth and all that is a part of it, really should not be and, at bottom, is devoid of true Being . . . The deepest aversion to time does not consist of the mere degradation of the earthly. For Nietzsche, the most profound revenge consists of that reflection which posits eternal Ideals as the absolute, compared with which the temporal must degrade itself to actual non-being.

How is man to assume dominion over the earth, how is he to take the earth, as earth, into his guardianship, if and as long as he degrades the earthly in that the spirit of revenge determines his reflection! If saving the earth as earth is at stake, then the spirit of revenge must first vanish. That is why deliverance from the spirit of revenge is the bridge to the highest hope for Zarathustra." [60]

---

[60] *Ibid.*, pp. 116–117: "Nietzsche bestimmt die Rache als 'des Willens Widerwille gegen die Zeit und ihr 'Es war.'' Diese nachgetragene Bestimmung hebt nicht einen vereinzelten Charakter der Zeit unter Vernachlässigung der beiden anderen einseitig heraus, sondern sie kennzeichnet den Grundzug der Zeit in ihrem ganzen und eigentlichen Zeitwesen. Mit dem 'und' in der Wendung 'die Zeit und ihr 'Es war'' leitet Nietzsche nicht zu einer blossen Anfügung eines besonderen Zeitcharakters über. Das 'und' bedeutet hier so viel wie; und das heisst. Rache ist des Willens Widerwille gegen die Zeit und das heisst: gegen das Vergehen und sein Vergängliches. Dieses ist für den Willen solches, wogegen er nichts mehr ausrichten kann, woran sein Wollen sich ständig stösst. Die Zeit und ihr 'Es war' ist der Stein des Anstosses, den der Wille nicht wälzen kann. Die Zeit als Vergehen ist das Widrige, an dem der Wille leidet. Als so leidender Wille wird er selbst zum Leiden am Vergehen, welches Leiden dann sein eigenes Vergehen will und damit will, dass überhaupt alles wert sei, zu vergehen. Der Widerwille gegen die Zeit setzt das Vergängliche herab. Das Irdische, die Erde und alles, was zu ihr gehört, ist das, was eigentlich nicht sein sollte und im Grunde auch kein wahres Sein hat . . . Der tiefste Widerwille gegen die Zeit besteht aber nicht in der blossen Herabsetzung des Irdischen. Die tiefste Rache besteht für Nietzsche in jenem Nachdenken, das überzeitliche Ideale als die

It is clear from this that deliverance from the spirit of revenge is a necessary condition for man' dominion over the earth, for the realization of the overman.

Yet, of what does this deliverance from aversion to transience consist? In a liberation from the will itself? In Schopenhauer's sense and that of Buddhism? To the extent that the Being of beings is will in modern metaphysical theory, deliverance from the will would, simultaneously, be deliverance from Being, a fall into empty nothingness. To Nietzsche deliverance from revenge is indeed deliverance from what is repugnant, resistant and degrading in the will, but not a release from all willing. Deliverance liberates aversion from its *No* and frees it for a Yes. What does this *Yes* affirm? Precisely what the aversion of the spirit of revenge negates: time, transience.

This *Yes* to time is the will that would have transience abide, would not have it degraded to nihility. But how can transience abide? Only in such a way that, as transience, it does not just constantly pass, but always comes to be. It would abide only in such a way that transience and what ceases to be returns as the selfsame in its coming. But this recurrence itself is abiding only if it is eternal. According to metaphysical theory the predicate "eternal" belongs to the Being of beings.

Deliverance from revenge is the bridge from contempt for time, to the will that represents beings in the eternal recurrence of the same, in which the will becomes the advocate of the circle.

In other words: Only when the Being of beings is represented to man as the eternal recurrence of the same, only then can man cross the bridge and, crossing over, delivered from the spirit of revenge, can be the overman.[61]

---

absoluten ansetzt, an denen gemessen das Zeitliche sich selber zum eigentlich Nicht-Seienden herabsetzen muss.

Wie aber soll der Mensch die Erdherrschaft antreten können, wie kann er die Erde als Erde in seine Obhut nehmen, wenn er und solange er das Irdische herabsetzt, insofern der Geist der Rache sein Nachdenken bestimmt? Gilt es, die Erde als Erde zu retten, dann muss zuvor der Geist der Rache verschwinden. Darum ist für Zarathustra die Erlösung von der Rach die Brücke zur höchsten Hoffnung."

[61] *Ibid.*, pp. 117–118: "Doch worin besteht diese Erlösung vom Widerwillen gegen das Vergehen? Besteht sie in einer Berfreiung vom Willen überhaupt? Im Sinne Schopenhauers und des Buddhismus? Insofern nach der Lehre der neuzeitlichen Metaphysik das Sein des Seienden Wille ist, käme die Erlösung vom Willen einer Erlösung vom Sein und somit einem Fall in das leere Nichts gleich. Die Erlösung von der Rache ist für Nietzsche zwar die Erlösung vom Widrigen, vom Widersetzlichen und Herabsetzenden im Willen, aber keinswegs die Herauslösung aus allem Wollen. Die Erlösung löst den Widerwillen von seinem Nein und macht ihn frei für ein Ja. Was bejaht dieses Ja? Genau das was der Widerwille des Rachegeistes verneint: die Zeit, das Vergehen.

"Dieses Ja zur Zeit ist der Wille, das Vergehen bleibe und nicht in das Nich-

The initial question of the essay, Who is Nietzsche's Zarathustra?, thus receives an answer which is deceptive in its simplicity: "He is the teacher whose doctrine would liberate previous reflection from the spirit of revenge unto a Yes to the eternal recurrence of the same." [62]

As for the *nature* of eternal recurrence, Heidegger's commentary, voluminous though it be, comes finally to this: it is a vision and an enigma. But, for Heidegger, it is no *mere* enigma. As Nietzsche's fundamental thought, the doctrine of eternal recurrence shares the fate of all such revelations of Being; "that which is unique in what a thinker is able to express can neither be demonstrated nor refuted logically or empirically. Nor is it a matter of faith. It can only be made visible in questioning-thinking. What is then seen always appears as that which is always *worthy* of questioning . . . The eternal recurrence of the same remains a vision for him, but also an enigma. It can be neither verified nor refuted logically or empirically." [63]

For Heidegger, in the last analysis, the doctrine of eternal recurrence represents the highest expression of the will-to-power: "The highest will-to-power, that is, the life-force in all life, is to represent transience as a fixed Becoming within the eternal recurrence of the same, and so to render it secure and stable." [64]

tige herabgesetzt werde. Aber wie kann das Vergehen bleiben? Nur so, dass das Vergehen und sein Vergangenes in seinem Kommen als das Gleiche wiederkehrt. Diese Wiederkehr selbst ist jedoch nur dann eine bleibende, wenn sie eine ewige ist. Das Prädikat 'Ewigkeit' gehört nach der Lehre der Metaphysik zum Sein des Seienden.

"Die Erlösung von der Rache ist der Übergang vom Widerwillen gegen die Zeit zum Willen, der das Seiende in der ewigen Wiederkehr des Gleichen vorstellt, indem der Wille zum Fürsprecher des Kreises wird.

"Anders gewendet: erst wenn das Sein des Seienden als ewige Wiederkehr des Gleichen sich dem Menschen vorstellt, kann der Mensch über die Brücke hinübergehen und, erlöst vom Geist der Rache, der Hinübergehende, der Übermensch sein."

[62] *Ibid.*, p. 118: "Er ist der Lehrer, dessen Lehre das bisherige Nachdenken vom Geist der Rache in das Ja zur ewigen Wiederkehr des Gleichen befreien möchte."

[63] *Ibid.*, p. 119: "das Einzige, was jeweils ein Denker zu sagen vermag, lässt sich logisch oder empirisch weder beweisen noch wiederlegen. Es ist auch nicht die Sache eines Glaubens. Es lässt sich nur fragenddenkend zu Gesicht bringen. Das Gesichtete eracheint dabei stets als das Fragwürdige . . . Die Ewige Wiederkehr des Gleichen bleibt für Zarathustra Gesicht zwar, aber Rätsel. Sie lässt sich logisch oder empirisch weder beweisen noch wiederlegen."

[64] *Ibid.*, p. 120: "Der höchste Wille zur Macht, d.h. das Lebendigste alles Lebens ist es, das Vergehen als ständiges Werden in der ewigen Wiederkehr des Gleichen vorzustellen und es so ständig und beständig zu machen."

Several questions, deferred until now, arise in any attempt to evaluate Heidegger's interpretation of Nietzsche's doctrine of eternal recurrence. The questions belong to different logical, or better methodological, orders.

The first question involves an assessment of the evidence Heidegger presents as the basis for his interpretation. A question raised at this level might be, "Do the texts (*viz. Thus Spoke Zarathustra*) support the contention that the doctrine of eternal recurrence is designed to liberate previous reflection from the spirit of revenge, conceived as aversion to time and transience?" This is essentially a textual question.

The second question, related to the first, involves an assessment as to whether or not Heidegger's interpretation really sheds any light on the doctrine of eternal recurrence at all. We mean by this, does it answer the question which it initially posed; namely, the sense in which "eternal recurrence" is the *existentia* of the Being of beings, whose *essentia* is "will-to-power?"

The final question, a result of the preceding two, involves a judgment of the general context out of which Heidegger's interpretation is generated. The issue is to assess the adequacy of treating Nietzsche's doctrine of eternal recurrence as the *existentia* of the Being of beings. In short, does Heidegger's context emerge from Nietzsche's writings or are Nietzsche's works appropriated into an *a priori* context?

The three questions, although related, require different kinds of evidence before they can be adequately resolved. The first question requires only a contextual examination of the quotations Heidegger cites, to establish whether these quotations do in fact assert what Heidegger claims they do regarding the doctrine of eternal recurrence. The second question requires an analysis of the relationship between "will-to-power" and "eternal recurrence," as Heidegger interprets them, with a view to establishing whether anything new is contained in the interpretation of "eternal recurrence" which is not already contained in "will-to-power" and, thus, vindicates the claim that the two are *different* aspects of the Being of beings. The third and last question departs from a direct textual analysis, to the extent that it raises the general question of the adequacy of Heidegger's distinctions, *viz.*, "will-to-power" as the *essentia* of the Being of beings, "eternal recurrence" as its *existentia*. The evidence required, at that point, is in part contained in the previous chapter, concerning

Heidegger's view of the tradition. The issue here becomes whether or not it is convincing, on the basis of Nietzsche's own writings, to advance "The interpretation of the doctrine of eternal recurrence as the *last* 'metaphysical' position in Western thought?" [65] A treatment of this last question constitutes the final chapter of this study. It is obviously too large and too central a question to deal with in brief compass. It raises the problem of the historical adequacy of Heidegger's interpretation of Nietzsche's doctrine of eternal recurrence; the adequacy of his understanding of Nietzsche's "metaphysics," conditioned, as it is, by Heidegger's unique interpretation of the history of Western metaphysics as "nihilism" – the forgetfulness of Being. The first two questions, however, less ambitious but equally important as they are, can be dealt with in this chapter.

A central point of Heidegger's interpretation of the doctrine of eternal recurrence is that it is to liberate all reflection to-date from the spirit of revenge. Such a liberation is not merely an interesting metaphysical alternative, but a necessary historical requirement, as Heidegger conceives it, so that man may secure "the earth as earth." The overman alone can affirm the doctrine of eternal recurrence, because he is himself a bridge from vengeful reflection to liberated affirmation. Revenge is, as Heidegger reads Nietzsche, aversion to time, an aversion which has allegedly characterized the history of Western thought. Thus, the overman overcomes all previous reflection ("the representation of beings in their Being") by liberating his thinking from contempt for time "unto a Yes to the eternal recurrence of the same," rendering becoming stable and secure.

The evidence upon which Heidegger bases this interpretation rests, for the most part, on three quotations from Nietzsche's *Thus Spoke Zarathustra:* (1) "For *that man be delivered from revenge,* that is the bridge to the highest hope for me and a rainbow after long storms," [66] (2) "*The spirit of revenge,* my friends, has so far been the subject of man's best reflection," [67] (3) "This, yes this alone, is *revenge* itself: the will's aversion to time and its 'It was.'" [68] The first quotation is essential. Without it the relationship between "deliverance," "bridge," and "revenge," cannot be cogently established. By introducing the

---

[65] *Nietzsche,* vol. I, pp. 258–259: "Die Auslegung der Wiederkunftslehre als der *letzten* 'metaphysischen' Grundstellung im abendländischen Denken."

[66] Cf. note # 54.

[67] Cf. note # 55.

[68] Cf. note # 59.

concept of deliverance from revenge as a necessary condition for Zarathustra's "highest hope," it leads to the next two quotations as equally necessary conditions for the fulfillment of "the highest hope." "Revenge" has dominated previous reflection. Its nature is "aversion to time and its 'It was.'" The three quotations, taken together, allow Heidegger the latitude he needs to claim that "Nietzsche sees the nature and significance of revenge metaphysically." [69] This is important because Heidegger is anxious to establish the view that the doctrine of eternal recurrence is a metaphysical, not a "moral" or "psychological" concept. The thrust of Heidegger's very fine essay "Who is Nietzsche's Zarathustra?", is not intent upon subsuming the psychological and ethical under the metaphysical. Rather, Heidegger seems to see it as an either/or: Revenge and the doctrine of eternal recurrence are either metaphysical, or ethical and psychological concepts. "Revenge is here not a mere theme of morality nor is deliverance from revenge the task of moral education. Nor is revenge and vengefulness an object of psychology." [70]

I shall maintain in what follows that, at best, Heidegger's emphasis is mistaken. The three quotations which he cites, when seen in their context, reveal that Nietzsche, at a minimum, *is* speaking of revenge in "ethical" and "psychological" terms. Whether the concept of revenge is also "metaphysical" we leave as an open question.

The quotation "For *that man be delivered from revenge,* that is the bridge to the highest hope for me and a rainbow after long storms," occurs in the Second Part of *Thus Spoke Zarathustra,* in a section titled "On the Tarantulas." The "tarantulas" are the vengeful ones. Their revenge finds expression through the preaching of equality. "Thus I speak to you in a parable – you who make souls whirl, you preachers of *equality!*" [71] The point, here, is that Heidegger need not have gone far to discover that Nietzsche's plea for deliverance from the spirit of revenge was directed, in the section from which he quotes, at the preachers of equality (*not* the history of "metaphysics"). Moreover, if Heidegger had continued quoting the passage he selected, he

---

[69] *Vorträge und Aufsätze,* p. 112: "Wesen und Tragweite der Rache sieht Nietzsche metaphysisch."

[70] Cf. note # 58.

[71] Karl Schlechta (ed.) *Werke in drei Bänden,* vol. II (München: Hanser, 1955), p. 357: "Also rede ich zu euch im Gleichnis, die ihr die Seelen drehend macht, ihr Prediger der *Gleichheit!*"

would have noted that Nietzsche's critique is both "moral" and "psychological" in intention, meaning, and tone.

For *that man be delivered from revenge,* that is the highest hope for me and a rainbow after long storms.

The tarantulas, of course, would have it otherwise. "What justice means to us is precisely that the world be filled with the storms of our revenge" – thus they speak to one another.

"We shall wreak vengeance and abuse upon all whose equals are we not" – thus do the tarantula-hearts vow.

"And 'will to equality' shall henceforth be the name for virtue; and against all that has power we want to raise our clamor!"

You preachers of equality, the tyrannomania of impotence clamors thus out of you for equality: your most secret ambitions to be tyrants thus shroud themselves in words of virtue!

Aggrieved conceit, repressed envy – perhaps the conceit and envy of your fathers – erupt from you as a flame and as the frenzy of revenge.[72]

The context in which Nietzsche's "highest hope" for deliverance from revenge occurs is clearly "moral-psychological." Nietzsche opposes the "preachers of equality," in "On the Tarantulas," in the same polemical tone in which he rejected all "slave moralities." The struggle for equality is, for Nietzsche, an expression of the will to dominate – "the tyrannomania of impotence." Those who loudly advocate equality are, for Nietzsche, fundamentally powerless, and in their impotence disguise their lust for power as virtue – "your most secret ambitions to be tyrants thus shroud themselves in words of virtue!" Equally important for our purposes, Nietzsche assesses this advocacy of equality, which is a disguised will to dominate, in psychological

---

[72] *Ibid.*, p. 357: "Denn *dass der Mensch erlöst werde von der Rache:* das ist mir die Brücke zur höchsten Hoffnung und ein Regenbogen nach langen Unwettern.

"Aber anders wollen es freilich die Taranteln. 'Das gerade heisse uns Gerechtigkeit, dass die Welt voll werde von den Unwettern unser Rache' – also reden sie miteinander.

"'Rache wollen wir üben und Beschimpfung an allen, die uns nicht gleich sind' – so geloben sich die Tarantel-Herzen.

"'Und, Wille zur Gleichheit' – dass selber soll fürderhin der Name für Tugend werden; und gegen alles, was Macht hat, wollen wir unser Geschrei erheben!'

"Ihr Prediger der Gleichheit, der Tyrannen-Wahnsinn der Ohnmacht schreit also aus euch nach Gleichheit: eure heimlichsten Tyrannen-Gelüste vermummen sich also in Tugend-Worte!

"Vergrämter Dünkel, verhaltener Neid: aus euch bricht's als Flamme heraus und Wahnsinn der Rache."

terms; as revenge. "Aggrieved conceit, repressed envy . . . erupt from you as a flame and as the frenzy of revenge."

To be sure, the fact that Nietzsche's "highest hope" is responsive to an alleged "moral" and "psychological" *condition humaine* does not answer the question of the *nature* of deliverance from revenge. So Heidegger is perhaps justified in ignoring the context of his first citation to some extent. But if the hope for "deliverance from revenge" emerges within a "moral" and "psychological" perspective, perhaps deliverance itself moves in the same sphere. Heidegger, of course, thinks otherwise.

Heidegger makes two important claims about the nature of deliverance from revenge. The first is that revenge has characterized all reflection to-date. The second is that revenge is aversion to time as such. In Heidegger's treatment the "moral" and "psychological" dimension disappear, while "revenge" is treated as a metaphysical notion.

"*The spirit of revenge,* my friends has so far been the subject of man's best reflection; and wherever there was suffering, there punishment was also wanted."
This sentence relates revenge at the outset to all of mankind's reflection to this date. Here reflection means not just any pondering, but that thinking in which man's relation to what is, to all beings, is grounded and attuned. In so far as man relates to beings, he represents being with reference to the fact that it is, what and how it is, how it might be and ought to be; in short, he represents being with reference to its Being. This representation is thinking.
According to Nietzsche's statement, that representation has so far been determined by the spirit of revenge.[73]

Heidegger interprets Nietzsche's "revenge" as the pervasive and sustaining spirit of all previous reflection, the representation of beings

---

[73] *Vorträge und Aufsätze,* pp. 111–112: " '*Der Geist der Rache:* Meine Freunde, das war bisher der Menschen bestes Nachdenken; und wo Leid war, da sollte immer Strafe sein.'
Durch diesen Satz wird die Rache im vorhinein auf das ganze bisherige Nachdenken der Menschen bezogen. Das hier genannte Nachdenken meint nicht irgend ein Überlegen, sondern jenes Denken, worin das Verhältnis des Menschen zu dem beruht und schwingt, was ist, zum Seienden. Insofern der Mensch sich zum Seienden verhält, stellt er das Seiende hinsichtlich dessen vor, dass es ist, was es und wie es ist, wie es sein möchte und sein soll, kurz gesagt: das Seiende hinsichtlich seines Seins. Dieses Vor-stellen ist das Denken.
Nach dem Satz Nietzsches wird dieses Vortellen bisher durch den Geist der Rache bestimmt."

in their Being, which Heidegger calls "thinking." Deliverance from revenge is thus a deliverance from the pervasive spirit of previous thought, through the eclipse of aversion to time.

Nietzsche defines revenge as "the wills aversion to time and its 'It was'." That appended definition does not single out one characteristic of time by neglecting the other two. Rather, it identifies the foundation of time in its entire and intrinsic time-essence. Nietzsche's "and" in "time and its 'It was'," is not simply a transition to an additional specific feature of time. "And" here is the same thing as "and that means." Revenge is the will's aversion to time, and that means the ceasing to be and its transience. The will no longer has any influence over it and its willing constantly runs up against it. Time and its "it was" is the stumbling-block which the will cannot budge. Time, as transience, is the adversity which the will suffers. As suffering will, it suffers transience, wills its own cessation as suffering and, thereby, wills the disappearance of all things. The aversion to time degrades the transient. The earthly, the earth and all that is a part of it really should not be and, at bottom, is devoid of true Being . . .[74]

A noteworthy factor in Heidegger's interpretation of the material he quotes from Nietzsche [that the spirit of revenge has dominated previous reflection and that its nature is aversion to time as such] is its error of *omission*. The difficulty is not so much what Heidegger says about what he quotes, but what he ignores.[75] In the case of the three quotations Heidegger cites as evidence for his interpretation of the doctrine of eternal recurrence, he ignores four factors. (1) Deliverance from revenge, as Zarathustra's highest hope, is a plea for deliverance from the "tarantula" slave morality and psychology. (2) Nietzsche defines "revenge" and "deliverance" in the very passages Heidegger selectively quotes. In each case the definition falls, at a minimum, into the sphere of philosophical psychology and morality – not only metaphysics. (3) "Time," as Nietzsche uses that term, doesn't refer primarily to "the foundation of time in its entire and intrinsic time-essence." Once again Nietzsche's point is directed toward the attitude we ought to take toward our lives, our deeds, our *past*. (4) When Nietzsche says that *"the spirit of revenge,* my friends, has so far been the subject of man's best reflection,"* he refers to the tendency to view existence as trial and punishment. His reference is not to

---

[74] Cf. note # 60.

[75] The same "selective" reading appears in his treatment of other figures in the tradition, as, for example, in the case of Plato and Descartes – cf. the previous chapter.

"thinking," understood as the representation of beings in their Being. He refers to the "madness" of treating existence as a half-way house – which has allegedly characterized the Judaeic-Christian tradition. If we quote, at length, the material Heidegger only partially quotes, the above points will become clearer.

To liberate those who lived in the past and to recreate all "it was" into a "thus I willed it!" – that alone should I call deliverance!

Will – that is the name of the liberator and joy-bringer; thus I taught you, my friends! But now learn this too: the will itself is still a prisoner.

Willing liberates; but what is it that puts even the liberator himself in fetters?

"It was" – that is the name of the will's gnashing of teeth and most secret melancholy. Powerless against what has been done, he is angry spectator of all that is past.

The will cannot will backward; and that he cannot break time and time's covetousness, that is the will's loneliest melancholy.

Willing liberates; what means does the will devise for himself to get rid of his melancholy and to mock his dungeon?

Alas, every prisoner becomes a fool! The imprisoned will liberate himself foolishly.

That time does not run backwards, that is his wrath; "that which was" is the name of the stone he cannot budge.

And so he moves stones out of wrath and displeasure and he wreaks revenge on whatever does not feel wrath and displeasure as he does.

Thus the will, the liberator, took to hurting; and on all who can suffer he wreaks revenge for his inability to go backwards.

This, yes this alone, is *revenge* itself; the will's aversion to time and its "it was."

Verily, a great follow dwells in our will; and it has become a curse for everything human that this folly has acquired spirit!

The spirit of revenge, my friends, has so far been the subject of man's best reflection; and wherever there was suffering punishment was also wanted.

For "punishment" is what revenge calls itself; with a hypocritical lie it creates a good conscience for itself.

Because there is suffering in those who will, insofar as they cannot will backwards, willing and all life were supposed to be – a punishment!

And now cloud upon cloud rolled over the spirit, until eventually madness preached "Everything passes away; therefore everything deserves to pass away!

"And this too is justice, this law of time that it must devour its children." Thus preached madness.

"Things are ordered morally according to justice and punishment. Alas, where is deliverance from the flux of things and from the punishment called existence?" Thus preached madness.

"Can there be deliverance if there is eternal justice? Alas, the stone *It was* cannot be moved: all punishments must be eternal too!" Thus preached madness.

No deed can be annihilated: how could it be undone by punishment! This, this is what is eternal in the punishment called existence, that existence must eternally become deed and guilt again!

"Unless the will should at last redeem himself and willing should become not willing." But, my brothers, you know this fable of madness!

I led you away from these fables when I taught you, "The will is a creator." All "it was" is a fragment, an enigma, a dreadful accident — until the creative will says to it, "But thus I willed it!"

Until the creative will says to it "But thus I will it! Thus shall I will it!" [76]

---

[76] *Werke in drei Bänden*, vol. II, pp. 394–395: "Die Vergangnen zu erlösen und alles 'Es war' umzuschaffen in ein 'So wollte ich es!' das hiesse mir erst Erlösung!

Wille — so heisst der Befreier und Freudebringer: also lehrte ich euch meine Freunde! Aber nun lernt dies hinzu: der Wille selber ist noch ein Gefangener.

Wollen befreit: aber wie heisst das, was auch den Befreier noch in Ketten schlägt?

'Es war': also heisst des Willens Zähneknirschen und einsamste Trübsal. Ohnmächtig gegen das, was getan ist — ist allem Vergangenen ein böser Zuschauer.

Nicht zurück kann der Wille wollen; dass er die Zeit nicht brechen kann und der Zeit Begierde — das ist des Willens einsamste Trübsal.

Wollen befreit: was ersinnt sich das Wollen selber, dass es los seiner Trübsal werde und seines Kerkers spotte?

Ach, ein Narr wird jeder Gefangene! Närrisch erlöst sich auch der gefangene Wille.

Dass die Zeit nicht zurückläuft, das ist sein Ingrimm; 'das, was war' — so heisst der Stein, den er nicht wälzen kann.

Und so wälzt er Steine aus Ingrimm und Unmut und übt Rache an dem, was nicht gleich ihm Grimm und Unmut fühlt.

Also wurde der Wille, der Befreier, ein Wehetäter: und an allem, was leiden kann, nimmt er Rache dafür, dass er nicht zurück kann.

Dies, ja dies allein ist *Rache* selber: des Willens Widerwille gegen die Zeit und ihr 'Es war.'

Wahrlich, eine grosse Narrheit wohnt in unserm Willen; und zum Fluche wurde es allem Menschlichen, dass diese Narrheit Geist lernte!

Der Geist der Rache, meine Freunde, das war bisher der Menschen bestes Nachdenken; und wo Leid war, da sollte immer Strafe sein.

'Strafe' nähmlich, so heisst sich die Rache selber: mit einem Lügenwort heuchelt sie sich ein gutes Gewissen.

Und weil im Wollenden selber Leid ist, darob, dass er nicht zurück wollen kann — also sollte Wollen selber und alles Leben — Strafe sein!

Und nun wälzt sich Wolke auf Wolke über den Geist" bis endlich der Wahnsinn predigte: "Alles vergeht, darum ist alles wert zu vergehen!"

'Und dies ist selber Gerechtigkeit, jenes Gesetz der Zeit, dass sie ihre Kinder fressen muss': also predigte der Wahnsinn.

'Sittlich sind die Dinge geordnet nach Recht und Strafe. O wo ist die Erlösung

In Heidegger's interpretation of "On the Tarantulas," he ignored the fact that Nietzsche's plea for deliverance from the spirit of revenge is a response to the "tarantula" slave morality and psychology. In his interpretation of "On Deliverance," Heidegger's treatment is equally partial and incomplete.

Nietzsche defined what he meant by deliverance at the very outset of the quoted passage: "To liberate those who lived in the past and to recreate all 'it was' into a 'thus I willed it!' – that alone should I call deliverance." The same point is made once again at the conclusion of the quoted passage, when Nietzsche has Zarathustra say, "I led you away from these fables when I taught you, 'The will is a creator." All 'it was' is a fragment, an enigma, a dreadful accident – until the creative will says to it: But thus I willed it!' Until the creative will says to it 'But thus I will it! Thus shall I will it!' " Nietzsche's point is psychological, moral and, perhaps, metaphysical. The transformation of "it was" into a "thus I willed it" constitutes freedom from the spirit of evasion. His point, once again, is that our fate ought to be embraced with love; *amor fati*. Nietzsche's plea is addressed to the individual's attitude (psychological) towards himself and his world. The individual's life, deeds, despair and suffering, ought to be embraced because they are shaped by nothing alien. Man's role is a "free" creation to the extent that there are no known determining forces (his past) which shape his life.[77]

vom Fluss der Dinge und der Strafe 'Dasein?'' Also predige der Wahnsinn.

'Kann es Erlösung geben, wenn es ein ewiges Recht gibt? Ach, unwälzbar ist der Stein 'Es war': ewig müssen auch alle Strafen sein!' Also predigte Wahnsinn.

'Keine Tat kann vernichtet werden: wie könnte sie durch die Strafe ungetan werden! Dies, dies ist das Ewige an der Strafe 'Dasein,' dass das Dasein auch ewig wieder Tat und Schuld sein muss!

'Es sei denn, dass der Wille endlich sich selber erlöst und Wollen zu Nicht-Wollen würde –': doch ihr kennt, meine Brüder, dies Fabellied des Wahnsinn!

Weg führte ich euch von diesen Fabelliedern, als ich euch lehrte: 'der Wille ist ein Schaffender.'

Alles 'Es war' ist ein Bruchstück, ein Rätsel, ein grauser Zufall – bis der schaffende Wille dazu sagt: 'aber so wollte ich es!'

Bis der schaffende Wille dazu sagt: 'aber so will ich es! So werde ich's wollen!' "

[77] The emphasis is, indeed, on the fact that the forces which shape our destinies are unknown. The doctrine of eternal recurrence asserts that our lives recur eternally in an identical fashion and can recur in no other way. However, as was pointed out in the third chapter of this study, the doctrine of eternal recurrence – as an existential imperative – proclaims a paradox which suggests that I am "free" to create my determined fate. Bereft of any knowledge of what my life is and will be, I only know that my past is sealed for eternal recurrences.

But the will, unwilling to accept total responsibility for its past, its suffering, creates evasions for itself; "the will itself is still a prisoner." The will evades its creative authorship by its unwillingness to affirm its past. "'It was' – that is the name of the will's gnashing of teeth and most secret melancholy. Powerless against what has been done, he is angry spectator of all that is past. The will cannot will backward; and that it cannot break time and time's covetousness, that is the will's loneliest melancholy." In its melancholy unwillingness to accept the responsibility for its past, the will "becomes a fool." By a double lie the will devises a means "for himself to get rid of his melancholy and to mock his dungeon." What is the evasion? The "fable" – metaphysics and religion.[78] Metaphysics and religion function as palliatives which allow us the ultimate evasion of responsibility for our lives, by treating life itself as "punishment." "*The spirit of revenge,* my friends, has so far been the subject of man's best reflection; and wherever there was suffering, punishment was also wanted. For 'punishment' is what revenge calls itself; with a hypocritical lie it creates a good conscience for itself." So punishment is, in reality, hypocritical revenge against our past, our freedom. Unable, or better unwilling, to accept our lives as our own creation, unable to alter our past, the will contrives to see the past and existence itself morally and metaphysically. "Because there is suffering in those who will, insofar as they cannot will backwards, willing and all life were supposed to be – a punishment!" So the self-deceiving will began "until eventually madness preached." "Madness" preached that, since "everything passes away . . . everything deserves to pass away"; that "things are ordered morally according to justice and punishment"; that "all punishments must be eternal too!"; that "no deed can be annihilated . . . that existence must eternally become deed and guilt again!"

And although I cannot alter my past, my present and future emerge as open possibilities. My present and future are not sealed until I choose. Then, and then alone, does my present and future become a "fated" past. But to the extent that I "freely" will my being now and in the future, I also "freely" willed my past. "Thus I willed it!" And the recognition that one is the author of one's past is to bring to the individual the simultaneous awareness of his responsibility for the present and future. "Thus I will it! Thus shall I will it!" – This is, for Nietzsche, a "shattering" awareness – that we are not only responsible for our lives, without evasion, but that our existence could not be other than it is.

[78] There is a marked thematic similarity in this treatment of "fable" and in the treatment of "how the 'true world' finally becomes a fable" in *Twilight of the Idols,* presented in the third chapter of this study.

Finally, the will turned against itself, avenging itself against its own creative power by denying itself: "existence must eternally become deed and guilt again! Unless the will should at last redeem himself and willing should become not willing." Nietzsche may very well have had Schopenhauer's teaching in mind here, and he says of this non-willing: "But, my brothers, you know this fable of madness!"

Nietzsche's point, in "On Deliverance," is that the will must affirm and accept its own creative power, its accomplished past, its chosen present, and to-be-created future. To accomplish this it must overcome the moral-metaphysical fetters which preach surcease from the suffering of existence, which alienate doer from what is done, self from deeds, freedom from responsibility, by treating life, the senses, pain, passion, deception, as lamentable punishments for being incarcerated in a human body and world. "For *that man be delivered from revenge,* that is the bridge to the highest hope for me and a rainbow after long storms."

How does the above explication compare with Heidegger's? Heidegger's claim that Nietzsche sees revenge metaphysically and only metaphysically – neither psychologically nor morally – is either an arbitrary definition or is simply wrong. "Revenge is here not a theme of morality, nor is deliverance from revenge the task of moral education. Nor is revenge and vengefulness an object of psychology . . ."[79] "Nietzsche sees the nature and significance of revenge metaphysically."[80] Clearly Nietzsche does "see" revenge psychologically in the sections quoted above. Moreover, that Heidegger's definition of "metaphysical" adequately describes Nietzsche's "revenge" and "deliverance" is somewhat doubtful. When Nietzsche writes that the spirit of revenge has been the subject of man's best reflection, Heidegger takes this to mean that Nietzsche refers to "not just any pondering, but that thinking in which man's relation to what is, to all beings, is grounded and attuned . . . in short, he represents being with reference to its Being. This representation is thinking."[81] It is misleading, beyond terminological differences, to suggest that Nietzsche's references to metaphysics and religion as "madness" refers to a "thinking" which has traditionally represented "beings in their Being." Not only do beings lack any manner of Being (conceived either as *essentia* or as

---

[79] Cf. note #58 above for German.
[80] Cf. note #57 above for German.
[81] *Ibid.*

"self-disclosure") for Nietzsche, but he regarded the entire attempt to impose structure upon becoming as a hoax. If being's are "will-to-power," then metaphysical and religious doctrines imprison not only the world, beings, but first and foremost they keep human being in bondage. Nietzsche's emphasis upon the tradition's imprisonment of the creative will of the *individual* is almost totally absent in Heidegger's treatment. This finds its starkest expression in Heidegger's interpretation of the meaning of revenge as "the will's aversion to time and its 'It was.'" Heidegger explains: "Nietzsche says: revenge is the will's aversion. But 'will' signifies the Being of beings as a whole . . . By characterizing revenge as 'the will's aversion,' it retains its resistant persecution from the outset within the region of the Being of beings."[82] Is that an accurate characterization of the meaning of "will" in the section from which Heidegger quotes, "On Deliverance?" I think not. "'Thus I willed it!' – that alone should I call deliverance!", says Nietzsche. Is the will "ontological" (the Being of beings) or "humanistic" here? The sentence which immediately follows the one Heidegger quotes about the nature of revenge, leaves no room for doubt that Nietzsche refers to our human will. "Verily, a great folly dwells in our will; and it has become a curse for everything human that this folly has acquired spirit." Indeed, deliverance from revenge is not only liberation from the spirit of previous reflection, but the affirmation of a *creative* will against the distorted interpretations of "it was." "I led you away from all these fables when I taught you, 'The will is creator.' All 'it was' is a fragment, a dreadful accident – until the creative will says to it 'But thus I will it! Thus shall I will it!"

Do Nietzsche's quotations support or justify Heidegger's interpretation? Yes and no.

Deliverance from revenge *is* a bridge from contempt for time to the eternal recurrence of the same. But it is not primarily a "metaphysical" bridge; not an "ontological" deliverance; not a "metaphysical" time, nor an "ontological" revenge. Nietzsche's freedom from revenge is not, on the basis of the texts, a new representation of beings in their Being. Revenge is a lamentable human, all-too-human, will to find security, "psychological" security, in a painful, discordant,

---

[82] *Vorträge und Aufsätze,* p. 115: "Nietzsche sagt: Rache ist des Willens Widerwille. 'Wille' aber nennt das Sein des Seienden im Ganzen . . . Durch die Kennzeichnung der Rache als 'des Willens Widerwille' bleibt ihr widersetzliches Nachstellen zum voraus innerhalb des Bezugs zum Sein des Seienden.

frequently hostile, but for the most part indifferent universe. And this revenge, having acquired spirit, rails against man's fate by preaching religious and metaphysical doctrines in the form of evasive assurances. Metaphysics and religion are sublimated revenge against "becoming," offering release from the vicissitudes of life. Deliverance from the spirit of revenge thus requires not a new doctrine, but primarily a new man – indeed an *Übermensch*.

The second and last question concerning Heidegger's interpretation to be dealt with in this chapter is, "does his interpretation exhibit the sense in which eternal recurrence is the *existentia* of Being whose *essentia* is will-to-power?" The answer is a brief and unequivocal "no."

Heidegger is persuaded that eternal recurrence and will-to-power are two aspects of Being. "The two fundamental terms of Nietzsche's metaphysics, 'will-to-power' and 'eternal recurrence of the same,' determine beings in their Being in those aspects which have guided metaphysics since antiquity, *ens qua ens* in the sense of *essentia* and *existentia*." [83] One searches the texts in vain, however, for any compelling reason for suggesting this duality. Heidegger correctly suggests that "will-to-power" is not a "universal" which is distinguishable from its concrete expression. In Heidegger's interpretation, discussed above, beings *are* will-to-power. There is no ghost in the machine. But if "will-to-power" is manifest only in and as the concrete entity, as a "concrete universal," where does eternal recurrence enter? If "will-to-power" were a sort of "first principle" separate from the encountered world, one could perhaps construct an argument that the universal (transcendent) essence finds particular existential expression as eternal recurrence. But Heidegger had abandoned this option in interpreting will-to-power as present in, and definitive of, beings as beings. The logical conclusion of this position is, it seems to me, that with respect to will-to-power *essentia* and *existentia* are one. Hence if "will-to-power" designates the Being of beings it is an "existential essence." The *essentia* is the *existentia*. In what sense, then, is eternal recurrence an aspect of the Being of beings, its *existentia*?

Heidegger's suggested resolution has nothing to do with Nietzsche's writings. He suggests that since "eternal" is a predicate of the Being of beings in traditional metaphysics, Nietzsche too had to conceive the Being of beings under the guise of eternity. Since deliverance from

[83] Cf. note # 24 above for German.

revenge is designed to affirm transcience, Heidegger maintains that transience can abide "Only in such way that, as transience, it does not just constantly pass, but always comes to be. It would abide only in such a way that transience and what ceases to be returns as the selfsame in its coming. But this recurrence itself is abiding only if it is eternal. According to metaphysical theory, the predicate 'eternal' belongs to the Being of beings." [84] Strangely, "the will wills itself" as eternal recurrence because the predicate "eternal" is a traditional metaphysical predicate of Being. By implication, then, Nietzsche is a metaphysician who is destined to think within the traditional thought-pattern. It turns out, in this meta-textual interpretation, that Nietzsche, like all "old-fashioned" metaphysicians, can't really abide transience either . . . "this recurrence is abiding only if it is eternal." To take Heidegger's meta-textual interpretation one step further, Nietzsche's thinking too must at bottom be dominated by the spirit of revenge. And Heidegger, of course, claims *precisely* that. "What else remains for us to say but: Zarathustra's doctrine does not bring deliverance from revenge?" [85] It would appear that the basis for affirming the passage of all things, embracing one's past, present, future, and the world's, under the yoke of eternal recurrence, is that in Nietzsche's thinking "there is nonetheless concealed an aversion to mere transience and, therefore, a supremely spiritualized spirit of revenge." [86] Heidegger's ultimate basis for affirming this thesis rests, apart from the fact that it fits neatly into his view of the history of metaphysics,[87] upon a single entry from the *Nachlass,* GOA XIV 404. "A spirit strengthened by wars and victories, to whom conquest, adventure, danger, even pain have become a necessity; the habituation to sharp mountain air, to wintry walks, to ice and mountains in every

[84] *Vorträge und Aufsätze,* pp. 117–118: "Nur so, dass es als Vergehen nicht stets nur geht, sondern immer kommt. Nur so, dass das Vergehen und sein Vergangenes in seinem Kommen als das Gleiche wiederkehrt. Diese Wiederkehr selbst ist jedoch nur dann eine bleibende, wenn sie eine ewige ist. Das Prädikat 'Ewigkeit' gehört nach der Lehre der Metaphysik zum Sein des Seienden."

[85] *Ibid.,* p. 122: "Was bleibt uns anderes, als zu sagen: Zarathustra's Lehre bringt nicht die Erlösung von der Rache?"

[86] *Ibid.,* p. 121: "verbirgt sich . . . auch noch ein Widerwillen gegen das blosse Vergehen und somit ein höchst vergeistigter Geist der Rache."

[87] The entire notion that Nietzsche thinks the Being of beings as "will-to-power" and "eternal recurrence" will be examined in the next chapter. The conclusion will be that Nietzsche did not want to "think" "the Being of beings" at all.

sense; a sort of sublime malice and extreme exuberance of revenge – for there is *revenge* in it, revenge against life itself, when one who suffers greatly *takes life under his protection.*" [88] Heidegger takes this one note as the necessary evidence for maintaining the view that Nietzsche's affirmation of becoming, as eternal recurrence, is motivated by the spirit of revenge. This is an extremely questionable methodological approach. To begin, the thesis rests upon a single entry which, if interpreted in the way Heidegger intends it to be interpreted, finds no corollary in any other Nietzsche entry. Second, it comes from the *Nachlass*. In the first chapter of this study it was suggested that the unpublished notes ought to be used as clarifying evidence for the published reflections. In this case, Heidegger's thesis rests upon a single contradictory, not supporting, entry from the literary estate. Finally, the entry itself comes from the rough drafts of prefaces Nietzsche had prepared for *The Gay Science*. Nietzsche suppressed it in the published preface to *The Gay Science,* the work which precedes *Thus Spoke Zarathustra.*

In the light of the above, is Heidegger suggesting that we should accept a note suppressed by Nietzsche himself as evidence that Nietzsche's critique of metaphysics and religion [that both are governed by the spirit of revenge] is equally applicable to his own philosophy? Although Heidegger seems to suggest this, in reality he does not. He is not interested in refuting Nietzsche's doctrine by demonstrating that it commits the same fallacy it lays at the doorstep of its opponents. Heidegger maintains that the spirit of revenge governs Nietzsche's reflections "in order to bring into focus how much and in what way, even Nietzsche's thinking moves within the spirit of reflection to-date ... Thought up to now is metaphysics, and Nietzsche's thinking presumably brings it to an end." [89]

According to Heidegger Nietzsche secures becoming under the protection of eternal recurrence because, as a captive of the tradition of Western metaphysics, he was fated to think the Being of beings, will-to-power, under the guise of eternity. Only by conceiving the *existentia* of will-to-power as eternal recurrence could Nietzsche's thinking fulfill the demand of traditional metaphysics.

[88] GOA *Nachlass* XIV, 404.
[89] *Vorträge und Aufsätze*, p. 122: "um unseren Blick darauf zu wenden, dass und inwiefern auch Nietzsches Denken sich im Geist des bisherigen Nachdenkens bewegt ... ; In jedem Falle ist das bisherige Denken Metaphysik, und Nietzsche's Denken vollzieht vermutlich ihre Vollendung."

CHAPTER III

HEIDEGGER'S NIETZSCHE IN
CRITICAL PERSPECTIVE

It is exceedingly difficult to give a reasoned assessment of Heidegger's interpretation of Nietzsche's doctrine of eternal recurrence. There are several contributing factors.

Heidegger's long and frequently repetitious interpretation is *deceptively* simple. Early in "Who is Nietzsche's Zarathustra?", Heidegger interjects: "Of course, we could now break in with a crude explanation, and assert with undeniable correctness: in Nietzsche's language 'life' means the will-to-power as the fundamental characteristic of all beings, not only of man. What 'suffering" means Nietzsche states in the following words 'All that suffers wills (*will*) to live' (W.W. vi, 469), i.e., everything whose way is the will-to-power. This means: 'The formative powers collide' (xvi, 151). 'Circle' is the sign of the ring which flows back into itself, and so always achieves the recurring selfsame." [1] Heidegger is fully aware of the fact that this condensation can be compressed even further into what he calls a "definition." Therefore, his next sentence reads: "Accordingly, Zarathustra presents himself as the advocate of the fact that all being is will-to-power, which suffers as creative, colliding will, and thus wills itself in the eternal recurrence of the same." [2]

The reader of Heidegger's Nietzsche will be disappointed if he expects his labors to culminate in a clearer definition. From the analytic point of view, if Heidegger's interpretation were compressed into a

---

[1] *Vorträge und Aufsätze,* pp. 102–103: "Zwar könnten wir jetzt durch eine grobschlächtige Erklärung eingreifen und mit unbestreitbarer Richtigkeit sagen: 'Leben' bedeutet in Nietzsches Sprache: der Wille zur Macht als der Grundzug alles Seienden nicht nur des Menschen. Was 'Leiden' bedeutet, sagt Nietzsche in folgenden Worten: 'Alles, was leidet, will leben . . .' (W.W. vi, 469), d.h. alles, was in der Weise des Willens zur macht ist. Dies besagt: 'Die gestaltender. Kräfte stossen sich' (xvi, 151). "Kreis" ist das Zeichen des Ringes, dessen Ringen in sich selbst zurücklauft und so immer das wiederkehrende Gleiche erringt."

[2] Cf. note # 45, preceding chapter.

capsule summary it would coincide with the "crude" version. Heidegger is, of course, well aware of this himself. Everything depends on *how* one understands Nietzsche, thinks *along* with him, and little depends upon the discursive outcome of the journey. As Heidegger would have it, to authentically think the problem of the doctrine of eternal recurrence we would have to begin from the perspective which tries to think Being and its history – as concealment in metaphysics. Nietzsche should then be understood as the last chapter in this history.

Heidegger interprets Nietzsche out of the phenomenon of *Seinsvergessenheit,* the forgetfulness of Being. He is, in reality, more concerned with what Nietzsche did *not* say – and how this allegedly conditioned what he *did* say. "The 'doctrine' of a thinker is that which is left unsaid in what he says." [3] Heidegger is "endeavoring to comprehend and express not what another thinker thought/said, but what he did not think/say, could not think/say, and why he could not think/say it." [4]

He who objects to Heidegger's interpretation runs the risk, on Heidegger's terms, of missing the question of Being altogether, aiding and perpetuating the fall of Being further into oblivion. Like arguments from revelation, reason seems impotent. Yet, it is precisely this privileged perspective which makes Heidegger's interpretation both interesting and suspect. Like Hegel's history of philosophy, Heidegger's Nietzsche studies are often inseparable from the author's own position. It is almost impossible to draw the line as to where Heidegger ends and Nietzsche begins, as was pointed out in his treatment of "nihilism," "will" and "revenge."

Nietzsche wrote in an aphoristic style in conscious opposition to any "system." To the extent that systems tend to reduce experience to polarities of veridical and illusory, apparent and real, each aphorism represents a self-contained totality, reflecting the autonomy and richness of each moment within becoming. The aphorism, then, is written in conscious opposition to what Nietzsche viewed as the reductive tendency in metaphysics. Yet, Heidegger regards Nietzsche as a metaphysician *par excellence.* To be sure, Nietzsche is a metaphysician in Heidegger's sense because he completes the cycle of

[3] *Platons Lehre von der Wahrheit,* p. 5: "Die 'Lehre' eines Denkers ist das in seinem Sagen Ungesagte."

[4] William Richardson, *Heidegger: Through Phenomenology to Thought* (Martinus Nijhoff: The Hague, 1963), p. 22.

Being's dissimulation from *alétheia* to certitude, to will-to-power. Yet, Nietzsche's conception of metaphysics is seriously at odds with Heidegger's.

Nietzsche identifies metaphysics with otherworldliness, the pursuit of Being, of which the Christian version is perhaps his classic example. The section from *Thus Spoke Zarathustra* entitled "On the Afterworldly," applies equally to metaphysics and Christianity. Nietzsche playfully and perhaps simplistically identifies "metaphysical" and "after-worldly." In the aforesaid section Nietzsche says: "Believe me, my brothers: it was the body that despaired of the body and touched the ultimate walls with the fingers of a deluded spirit. Believe me brothers: it was the body that despaired of the earth and heard the belly of Being (*Sein*) speak to it . . . But 'that world' is well concealed from humans – that dehumanized inhuman world which is heavenly nothing: and the belly of Being does not speak to humans at all, except as a human."[5] Nietzsche's opposition to any philosophy which is guided by the question of Being, however "Being" is to be interpreted, was unequivocal: "Saying Yes to contradiction and strife, to *Becoming,* together with the radical rejection of even the concept '*Being*' – in this I must, in any case, acknowledge that which has the closest affinity to my thought hitherto."[6] Nietzsche's opposition to posing philosophic problems from the perspective of Being is a consequence of his conviction that such a context is bound to miss the truth about becoming; that it is unstructured will-to-power, that it possesses neither order, goal, nor purpose. Thus Heidegger's question concerning the meaning of Being is, for Nietzsche, a thoroughly "metaphysical" one.

It should be rather clear, if we reverse our standpoint for a moment and judge Heidegger by Nietzsche's standards, that Heidegger's Being-

---

[5] *Werke in Drei Bänden,* ed. Karl Schlechta (Hanser Verlag: München, 1955), vol. II, p. 298: "Glaubt es mir, meine Brüder! Der Leib war's, der am Leibe verzweifelte – der tastete mit den Fingern des betörten Geistes an die letzten Wände. Glaubt es mir, meine Brüder! Der Leib war's, der an der Erde verzweifelt – der hörte den Bauch des Seins zu sich reden . . . Aber 'jene Welt' ist gut verborgen vor dem Menschen, jene entmenschlichte Welt, die ein himmlisches Nichts ist; und der Bauch des Seins redet gar nicht zum Menschen, es sei denn als Mensch."

[6] GOA XV, *Ecce Homo,* 65: ". . . das Jasagen zu Gegensatz und Krieg, das *Werden,* mit radikaler Ablehnung auch selbst des Begriffs '*Sein*' – darin muss ich unter allen Umständen das mir Verwandteste anerkennen, was bisher gedacht worden ist."

question is an eminently metaphysical one. To be sure, Heidegger would object to the identification of the Being of beings with any traditional "Being" of metaphysics – the absolute, unconditioned and infinite ground of becoming. But, then again, Nietzsche is surely not a conventional "metaphysician" either. If Nietzsche's rejection of (Platonic) metaphysics makes him a "metaphysician," why doesn't Heidegger's rejection of Being – as "traditionally" understood – qualify him for the same title? Indeed, if Nietzsche inadvertently falls into traditional thought modes, doesn't the same thing happen to Heidegger as well?

The later Heidegger stresses the role of Being in its coming-to-pass in thought. Being is the "agent" which speaks through a philosopher: "Thought is, more simply, thought of Being. The genitive has two meanings. Thought is of Being, in so far as thought, eventuated by Being, belongs to Being. Thought is at the same time thought of Being in so far as thought listens to, heeds, Being. Listening to and belonging to Being, thought constitutes what it is in its essential origin. Thought is – this means, Being has always, in the manner of destiny, concerned itself about its nature, embraced it."[7] Thought owes its nature as a response to Being's self-disclosure: ". . . that which above all, 'is,' is Being. Thought brings to fulfillment the relation of Being to the nature of man, it does not make or produce this relation. Thought merely offers it to Being as that which has been delivered to itself in language . . . Thought, on the other hand, lets itself be called into service by Being in order to speak the truth of Being."[8] Whatever else may be said about the initiative of Being, it certainly seems to carry with it the Nietzschean overtones of "metaphysics."

The later Heidegger treats Being, more often than not, as equiva-

---

[7] *Platons Lehre von der Wahrheit mit einem Brief über den "Humanismus,"* (Francke Verlag: Bern, 1947), pp. 56–57: "Das Denken, schlicht gesagt, ist das Denken des Seins. Der Genetiv sagt Zweifaches. Das Denken ist des Seins, insofern das Denken, vom Sein ereignet, dem Sein gehört. Das Denken ist zugleich Denken des Seins, insofern das Denken, dem Sein gehörend, auf das Sein hört. Als das hörend dem Sein gehörende ist das Denken, was es nach seiner Wesensherkunft ist. Das Denken ist – dies sagt: das Sein hat sich je geschicklich seines Wesens angenommen."

[8] *Ibid.,* pp. 53–54: "Was jedoch vor allen 'ist,' ist das Sein. Das Denken vollbringt den Bezug des Seins zum Wesen des Menschen. Es macht und bewirkt diesen Bezug nicht. Das Denken bringt ihn nur als das, was ihm selbst vom Sein übergeben ist, dem Sein dar. Dieses Darbieten besteht darin, dass im Denken das Sein zur Sprache kommt . . . Das Denken dagegen lässt sich vom Sein in den Anspruch nehmen, um die Wahrheit des Seins zu sagen."

lent to the history of Western thought, and as eschatological in its nature. Being, which is fatefully forgotten in metaphysics, would seem to have fated itself into forgetfulness. Whereas Heidegger viewed Being as dependent upon man, *Dasein,* in 1927 (*Being and Time*), there is a gradual but sharp reversal in his thought from 1930–1947, which becomes explicit in the *Letter on "Humanism."* Heidegger increasingly views man as dependent upon Being, as the caretaker and shepherd of Being. Nietzsche's orientation, in contradistinction to Heidegger's, is, of course, avowedly and perhaps even frantically humanistic. There is a sense in which Nietzsche is almost a belated "Renaissance" thinker. It is as if he were frantically eliminating any remnant of "otherworldliness," even its subtle retention in "naturalistic" metaphysics, in the name of a new humanism. In this sense, Heidegger's quest for Being seems much more a continuation of an older tradition.

Now if it is misleading to characterize Heidegger as a metaphysician, why is Heidegger's characterization of Nietzsche as a "metaphysician" compelling? To resolve this problem, it seems to me, we must turn the question of Being aside, assume the attitude of "conventional" scholarship i.e., proceed from the *texts* without the imposition of an *a priori* interpretive context, and ask whether or not Heidegger's interpretation – suggestive though it is – is plausible.

It is to Heidegger's credit that he tries to interpret the doctrine of eternal recurrence metaphysically i.e., as a theory about the nature of beings as such. For entirely too long scholars have stressed the eternal recurrence as a cosmological hypothesis, without obvious connection to the human predicament. Yet, the evidence suggests that Nietzsche was not entirely content with his own formulation of the eternal recurrence as a cosmological hypothesis.[9] Although Nietzsche tried to formulate the concept in cosmological terms, this plan never fully succeeded. The references which explore the cosmological dimension of the doctrine of eternal recurrence are few indeed – and none of them were published by Nietzsche. But Nietzsche did not merely choose to withhold these entries from publication. A critical examination of the entries supports the claim that Nietzsche had some doubts about the finality of the doctrine of eternal recurrence as a cosmological hypothesis. This is not to suggest that Nietzsche did not want to ground the eternal recurrence in a cosmology. The point is,

[9] Cf. Chapter II, Part I.

rather, that Nietzsche was *led* to the (unsatisfactory) cosmological interpretation as a consequence or corollary of its "existential" inception. It seems reasonable to suggest that Nietzsche was struck by the eternal recurrence because of its effect upon man's understanding of himself: "Even if the circular repetition is only a probability or possibility, even the thought of a possibility can shatter and transform us – not only experiences and definite expectations! How the (mere) possibility of eternal damnation has worked." [10] "My doctrine declares that you must wish to live again – you will *anyway*!" [11]

Although Heidegger is to some extent justified in failing to stress the cosmological interpretation of eternal recurrence, it does not follow from this that he is justified in ignoring it altogether, which, of course, he does.

If Nietzsche explored the possibility of the doctrine of eternal recurrence as a cosmological hypothesis as a result of the belief that it could "shatter and transform us," one is justified in asking for a clarification of its existential (not necessarily ontological) consequences. It is at this point that Heidegger's interpretation is weakest, in my opinion. His interpretation is inadequate in at least five ways. First, besides ignoring the cosmological dimension, Heidegger fails to seriously consider the doctrine of eternal recurrence as a critique of the specifically Christian *weltanschauung*. Second, and as a consequence of the first, Heidegger misconstrues the nature of Nietzsche's anti-Platonism, as a consequence of which, third, he distorts Nietzsche's conception of nihilism. Fourth, Heidegger ignores the existential ("axiological") intention of the doctrine of eternal recurrence, as a consequence of which, fifth, he misinterprets the meaning of the "moment" in Nietzsche's thought.

The dialectic of the doctrine of eternal recurrence functions as an affirmation of becoming. For Nietzsche, metaphysics and Christianity had formed an alliance, as it were, against becoming:

1. The true world; attainable for the sage, the pious, the virtuous one – he lives in it, *he is it*. (Oldest form of the idea, relatively clever, simple, persuasive. Circumlocution for the sentence, "I, Plato, *am* the truth!).

2. The true world; unattainable for now, but promised for the sage, the pious, the virtuous one ("for the sinner who repents"). (Progress of the

[10] Cf. note # 3, Chapter III, Part I for German.
[11] Cf. note # 5, Chapter III, Part I.

idea: it becomes more subtle, deceptive, incomprehensible – it becomes female, it becomes Christian . . .)" [12]

The true world is an "error" for Nietzsche because it destroys precisely what it seeks to value: life. "Any distinction between a 'true' and an 'apparent' world –whether in the Christian manner or in the manner of Kant (in the end, an *underhanded* Christian) – is only a suggestion of decadence, a symptom of the *decline of life*." [13]

Nietzsche diagnosed the origin of the dissimulation of experience – the body, senses, and spirit – as rooted in the affirmation of the primacy of reason: "All that philosophers have handled for thousands of years have been concept-mummies; nothing real escaped their grasp alive. When these honorable idolators of concepts worship something, they kill it and stuff it; they threaten the life of everything they worship. Death, change, old age, as well as procreation and growth, are to their minds objections – even refutations . . ." [14] Nietzsche regards the ultimate category of this concept-worship as symbolized by the "God" of the philosophers (or alternatively Being, Absolute, etc.). "Thus they arrive at their stupendous concept 'God.' That which is last, thinnest and emptiest is put first." [15] Ignoring Nietzsche's intentional oversimplifications, we are led to a clearer conception of what he wants to affirm: "The 'apparent' world is the only one: the 'true' world is merely *added by a lie*." [16]

Nietzsche rejects all antagonism toward unbridled, unrestrained becoming, with vitriolic simplicity. Consequently, the artist appears as an ideal type, for Nietzsche, because he intensifies, affirms, and deepens appearance: "For 'appearance' in this case means reality

[12] GOA VIII *Die Götzendämmerung,* 82. For German cf. Chapter III, Part I, note # 13.

[13] *Werke in Drei Bänden,* (ed.) Karl Schlechta (Hanser Verlag: München, 1955), Vol. II, p. 961: "Die Welt scheiden in eine 'wahre' und eine 'scheinbare,' sei es in der Art des Christentums, sei es in der Art Kants (eines *hinterligsten* Christen zu guter Letzt –) ist nur eine Suggestion der *decadence* – ein Symptom *niedergehenden* Lebens . . ."

[14] *Ibid.,* p. 957: "Alles, was Philosophen seit Jahrtausenden gehandhabt haben, waren Begriffs-Mumien; es kam nichts Wirkliches lebendig aus ihren Händen. Sie töten, sie stopfen aus, diese Herren Begriffs-Götzendiener, wenn sie anbeten – sie werden allem lebensgefährlich, wenn sie anbeten. Der Tod, der Wandel, das Alter ebensogut als Zeugung und Wachstum sind für sie Einwände – Widerlegungen sogar."

[15] *Ibid.,* p. 959: "Damit haben sie ihren stupenden Begriff 'Gott.' Das Letzte, Dünnste, Leerste wird als Erstes gesetzt . . ."

[16] *Ibid.,* p. 958: "Die 'scheinbare' Welt ist die einzige: die 'wahre Welt' ist nur *hinzugelogen*."

once more, only by way of selection, reinforcement and correction. The tragic artist is no pessimist: he is precisely the one who says *Yes* to everything questionable, even to the terrible – he is Dionysian."[17] But even Nietzsche recognized that the affirmation of becoming is by no means a necessary consequence of the destruction of the "true world." "The true world we have abolished: which world remained? The apparent one perhaps . . . But no! *With the true world we have abolished the apparent one as well!* (Noon; moment of the briefest shadow; end of the longest error; high point of humanity; INCIPIT ZARATHUSTRA)."[18]

It is of more than passing interest to note that Zarathustra, the teacher of the overman and eternal recurrence, appears *after* the true world and the apparent one have been abolished. Nietzsche does not destroy the "true world." On the contrary, he takes its destruction – symbolized as the death of God – to be an historical fact. The world of Ideas and Ideals has simply become irrelevant, from Nietzsche's standpoint. The highest values have been devalued. This is precisely the phenomenon of nihilism, as Nietzsche understood it. Although traditional metaphysics and Christianity had become irrelevant in the direction and evaluation of life, Nietzsche's contemporaries were not embued with a Dionysian spirit either. Rather, becoming represented an endless and meaningless flow toward a vague and uncritically assumed future goal. The idea of progress survived unscathed – and unexamined – in a Darwinist cosmos.

Nietzsche's problem, then, became one of re-valuing a becoming which had been further devalued. And, the concept of eternal recurrence constituted this revaluation.

For Nietzsche, the doctrine of eternal recurrence has a dual function. It is an antidote to Platonic-Christian "otherworldliness," as well as the nihilism implicit in the abolition of the "true world." Consequently, where Plato distinguishes the apparent and the real, stressing the logical and ontological priority of the latter, the apparent world becomes the plenary mode for Nietzsche. To redeem becoming from an aimless relativity, each moment of cosmic change is regarded as sacred. Becoming is valued *as* being, by Nietzsche: "To *stamp* the

---

[17] *Ibid.,* p. 961: "Denn 'der Schein' bedeutet hier die Realität *noch einmal,* nur in einer Auswahl, Verstärkung, Korrektur . . . Der tragische ist kein Pessimist – er sagt gerade *Ja* zu allem Fragwürdigen und Furchtbaren selbst, er ist *dionysisch.*"

[18] Cf. note # 13, Chapter III, Part I, for German.

character of being upon becoming – *that is the highest will-to-power.*"[19]

The degree to which Nietzsche transforms what he took to be Platonic-Christian values has not been sufficiently stressed by Nietzsche scholars. Not only is the dichotomy of the apparent and the real reversed by Nietzsche, but the absence of a doctrine of recollection (*anamnesis*) is central to the concept of eternal recurrence.[20]

The eternal recurrence functions, in the final analysis, as an existential imperative. Existence itself is to be regarded *sub specii aeternitatis*. If Kant's categorical imperative is purely formal, deontologized, Nietzsche's imperative heightens, intensifies – and eternalizes – the content of experience.

Heidegger correctly emphasizes the spirit of revenge as central to Nietzsche's conception of metaphysics. But the spirit of revenge, as a *psychological* aversion to time and transience, is equally motivated by Nietzsche's opposition to Christianity. The two, metaphysics and Christianity, are inextricably connected for Nietzsche. More often than not, Nietzsche's view of metaphysics is conditioned by his conception of Christian "otherworldliness." Heidegger, of course, does not see it in this way. That Christianity and metaphysics are conceived by Nietzsche as explicit expressions of a psychological need to find order, stability, security, and ultimate purpose in a fleeting becoming, is totally ignored by Heidegger. The concept of metaphysics as sublimation ("I, Plato, *am* the truth"), for example, does not appear in Heidegger's Nietzsche studies. In fact, the concept of sublimation, as such, does not merit discussion even once in the more than 1,200 pages Heidegger has devoted to a discussion of Nietzsche's thought to-date.

A case could be made that Nietzsche's simplistic generalizations about metaphysics are merely the application of his anti "slave morality" position to a new sphere. Just as Christian "virtues" are, for Nietzsche, grounded in the phenomenon of *ressentiment,* the metaphysical bifurcation of the "apparent" and the "real" is grounded in revenge. The structure remains the same, only the content differs. In the moral sphere, *ressentiment* arises out of the experience of powerlessness, dependency, lack of self-direction and self-control. It finds expression as contempt for the body, beauty, power. In the meta-

---

[19] Cf. note # 15, Chapter III, Part I, for German.
[20] Cf. Chapter III, Part I, for exposition of this view.

physical sphere, vengeance becomes aversion to transience, to be-coming; aversion to time and temporality.

The degree to which Nietzsche opposed metaphysics, as "Chris-tian," is reflected in the last line of the last book he wrote, *Ecce Homo:* "Have I been understood? *Dionysos versus the Crucified.*"[21] In this last reflection, Nietzsche compressed the foundation of his thought into a simple formula. In the light of this formula, it is quite probable that Nietzsche's critique of metaphysics, as Platonism, stems from the assimilation of metaphysics into a Christian world-view.

Heidegger's interpretation stresses Nietzsche's opposition to meta-physics without, however, seeing this opposition as grounded in the religious phenomenon. The difference, here, is one of emphasis. Heidegger sees Nietzsche's "God" as a symbol for the order of meta-physics. The death of God proclaims the devaluation of Being. Al-though this interpretation is in part correct, Heidegger misses an im-portant dialectical interplay: metaphysics is also dead, because "God" is dead. If "God," considered as a "religious" reality, is dead because metaphysics is dead, it is equally true – for Nietzsche – that meta-physics is dead because the "religious" reality is no longer viable, no longer credible.

It is Heidegger's inability to see the dialectical relation between the religious and the metaphysical (and the psychological and the ontological) in Nietzsche's thinking, which makes his interpretation of the doctrine of eternal recurrence less than persuasive. For exam-ple, Heidegger correctly suggests that "Deliverance liberates aversion from its *No* and frees it for a *Yes*. What does this Yes affirm? Precisely what the aversion of the spirit of revenge negates: time, transience."[22] This means that time, transience, must be affirmed against the spirit of revenge, which has allegedly dominated the Western tradition. Why this affirmation should take the form of an *eternal recurrence* is un-clear. Therefore, Heidegger adds: "Time would not abide in such a way that, as transience, it constantly passes, but abide in such a way that what ceases-to-be within transience returns as the selfsame in its coming. But this recurrence itself is abiding only if it is eternal."[23] If one asks *why* Nietzsche should have affirmed transience as en-

---

[21] *Werke in Drei Bänden,* (ed.) Karl Schlechta (Hanser Verlag: München, 1955), Vol. II, p. 1159: "Hat man mich verstanden? – *Dionysos gegen den Ge-kreuzigten.*"

[22] Cf. note # 61, preceding Chapter, for German.

[23] *Ibid.*

during, eternal, rather than fleeting, Heidegger supplies a meta-textual answer in the sentence which immediately follows the above-quoted one: "According to metaphysical theory the predicate 'eternal' belongs to the Being of beings."[24] The intention of this sentence is unmistakable. Nietzsche is fated to affirm transience under the auspices of eternal recurrence apparently on the *assumption* that he is a "metaphysician." The argument is circular: Nietzsche is a metaphysician because he thinks Being as eternal recurrence, and he thinks Being as eternal recurrence because he is a metaphysician. Heidegger assumes that Nietzsche "thinks of Being as time"[25] in the traditional manner which requires that "eternity" be predicated of Being – hence of time (transience). Heidegger's Nietzsche study proceeds, *a priori*, as "The interpretation of the doctrine of eternal recurrence as the *last* 'metaphysical' position in Western thought."[26]

The texts, in opposition to Heidegger, merely indicate that Nietzsche did not want to "think" Being at all. If we do not assume, with Heidegger, that Nietzsche was victimized and fated to think Being as eternal recurrence (if, in short, we ignore the context which the question of Being imposes upon us), then the doctrine can perhaps be meaningfully understood as the attempted ultimate affirmation of becoming. The eternal recurrence stamps the character of Being upon becoming. It is not Being itself. And, it stamps this character upon becoming in the name of life: "the task is to live in such a way that you must wish to live again . . ."[27] The purpose of the doctrine of eternal recurrence is to proclaim the "highest state which a philosopher can attain: to stand in dionysiac fashion related to existence – my formula for it is 'amor fati.'"[28]

Whereas Heidegger's "moment" consists of endeavoring to recall the advent of Being, which has allegedly been lost in traditional metaphysics, Nietzsche's "moment" requires the affirmation of this very instant unto eternity. "The doctrine of eternal recurrence as a hammer in the hand of the most powerful . . ."[29] poses the question: "Do you

---

[24] *Ibid.*

[25] *Nietzsche,* Vol. I (Pfullingen: Neske, 1961) p. 28: "das Sein als Zeit denken."

[26] *Ibid.,* pp. 258–259: "Die Auslegung der Wiederkunftslehre als der *letzten* 'metaphysischen' Grundstellung im abendländischen Denken."

[27] Cf. note # 70, Chapter III, Part I, for German.

[28] Cf. note # 74, Chapter III, Part I, for German.

[29] Cf. note # 75, Chapter III, Part I.

want this once more and innumerable times more . . ."[30] as "a doctrine strong enough to have the effect of breeding: strengthening the strong, paralyzing and breaking the worldweary."[31]

The eternal recurrence intensifies the moment by eternalizing it. Even as a "mere possibility" it exalts *this* world against all "beyonds," religious or metaphysical. The eternal recurrence of the same demands a Sisyphus who is jubilant in the affirmation of his fate as its response.

Heidegger's interpretation, on the other hand, evades the psychological, axiological and, ultimately, the existential significance of Nietzsche's doctrine of eternal recurrence. This is inevitable, given the context which Heidegger, in his interpretations, superimposes upon the thinkers of the past.

The history of Western man, as Heidegger views it, is the history of nihilism – the forgetting of the Being of beings. And the history of philosophy is the instrument, the mechanism as it were, which is both responsible for and responsive to Being's dissimulation. Within philosophy ("metaphysics") it is the dissimulation of truth from *alétheia* to correctness which is responsible for the devolution of Being. So, with an elegant simplicity, the "correspondence" theory of truth – allegedly presupposed from Plato to Nietzsche – destroys the primordial sense of Being which, in turn, determines the path of Western history as nihilism.

Since Heidegger's metahistory of philosophy maintains that the Being of beings appears as "will" in modern (post-Cartesian) metaphysics, Nietzsche expresses the culmination of this tradition. Nietzsche's "will-to-power" and "eternal recurrence" are the inevitable (*Geschicklich*) outcome of the Platonic tradition.

Since the categorial mode of thinking has become inadequate to retrieve the lost sense of Being, Heidegger's own thinking moves within the context bequeathed by Nietzsche. Heidegger's latest reflections, captured by his own interpretation of the tradition, get caught up in a vision in which he strives for a thinking which, in awaiting Being, is a non-willing and non-representing.

Scholar: But thinking, understood in the traditional way, as re-presenting is a kind of willing; Kant, too, understands thinking this way when he characterizes it as spontaneity. To think is to will, and to will is to think.
Scientist: Then the statement that the nature of thinking is something

---

[30] Cf. note # 76, Chapter III, Part I.
[31] Cf. note # 77, Chapter III, Part I.

other than thinking means that thinking is something other than willing.

Teacher: And that is why, in answer to your question as to what I really wanted from our meditation on the nature of thinking, I replied: I want non-willing . . .[32]

Scientist: With the best of will, I cannot re-present to myself this nature of thinking.

Teacher: Precisely because this will of yours and your mode of thinking as re-presenting prevent it.

Scientist: But then, what in the world am I to do?

Scholar: I am asking myself that too.

Teacher: We are to do nothing but wait.[33]

The fruits of Heidegger's search for the meaning of Being apparently leave us, as a last alternative, a striving for non-representational thinking which *is* a non-willing. Only in this way are we prepared to await the coming-to-pass, in thought, of the Being of beings. The author of *Being and Time* yields to mysticism in the end.

We are inevitably reminded of what Nietzsche's own harsh and exaggerated judgment might have been about this style of "thinking." Being cannot appear before thought " 'Unless the will should at last redeem himself and willing should become not willing.' But, my brothers, you know this fable of madness!" [34]

Heidegger's metahistory of philosophy recounts the saga of Being's retrogression. If the diagnosis is mistaken, and I have labored to show that it is, the cure will probably fail too. But, after all, it is Nietzsche who reminds us that the errors of great thinkers are to be valued more than the truths of little ones.

---

[32] *Gelassenheit* (Pfullingen: Neske, 1959), pp. 31–32: "G: Das Denken ist jedoch, in der überlieferten Weise als Vorstellen begriffen, ein Wollen; auch Kant begreift das Denken so, wenn er es als Spontaneität kennzeichnet. Denken ist Wollen und Wollen ist Denken.

"F: Die Behauptung, das Wesen des Denkens sei etwas anderes als Denken, besagt dann, das Denken sei etwas anderes als wollen.

"L: Darum antwortete ich Ihnen auch auf die Frage, was ich bei unserer Besinnung auf das Wesen des Denkens eigentlich wolle, dies: ich will das Nicht-Wollen."

[33] *Ibid.,* pp. 36–37: "F: Ich kann mir dieses Wesen des Denkens mit dem besten Willen nicht vorstellen.

"L: Weil gerade dieser beste Wille und die Art Ihres Denkens als Vorstellen Sie daran hindern.

"F: Was soll ich dann in aller Welt tun?

"G: Das frage ich mich auch.

"L: Wir sollen nichts tun sondern warten."

[34] Cf. note # 76, preceding chapter, for German.

BIBLIOGRAPHY

Allemann, Beda. *Hölderlin und Heidegger.* Zürich: Atlantis, 1956.

Aristotle. *The Basic Works of Aristotle.* R. McKeon (ed.) New York: Random House, 1941.

Bäumler, Alfred. *Nietzsche der Philosoph und Politiker.* Leipzig: Reclam, 1931.

Bertram, Ernest. *Nietzsche: Versuch einer Mythologie.* Berlin: Bondi, 1918.

Biemel, Walter. *Le Concept de Monde chez Heidegger.* Louvain & Paris: J. Vrin, 1950.

Birault, Henri. "Existence et vérité d'après Heidegger," *Revue de Métaphysique et de Morale,* LVI, 35–87. 1950.

Burnet, John. *Early Greek Philosophy.* London: A & A Black, Ltd., 1930.

Clark, Gordon H. *Selections from Hellenistic Philosophy.* New York: Appleton-Century-Crofts, 1940.

Coppleston, Frederick. *A History of Philosophy,* 7 vols. Maryland: Newman Press, 1946–1966.

Danto, Arthur. *Nietzsche as Philosopher.* New York & London: Macmillan, 1965.

Demske, James M. *Sein, Mensch und Tod.* Freiburg & München: Alber, 1963.

Descartes, René. *The Philosophical Works of Descartes,* 2 vols. Trans. Haldane and Ross. New York: Dover, 1955.

De Waelhens, Alphonse. *La philosophie de Martin Heidegger.* Louvain: Institut Supérieur de Philosophie, 1942.

Ewald, Oscar. *Nietzsches Lehre in ihren Grundbegriffen: Die Ewige Wiederkunft des Gleichen und der Sinn des Übermenschen.* Berlin: Hofmann, 1903.

Findlay, J. N. *Hegel: A Re-Examination.* New York: Collier Books, 1962.

Förster-Nietzsche, Elisabeth. *Das Leben Friedrich Nietzsches.* 3 vols. Leipzig: C. G. Naumann, 1895–1904.

Frings, Manfred S. (ed.). *Heidegger and the Quest for Truth.* Chicago: Quadrangle Books, 1968.

Fürstenau, Peter. *Heidegger: das Gefüge seines Denkens.* Frankfurt a/M: Klostermann, 1958.

Gray, J. Glenn. "Heidegger's Course: From Human Existence to Nature," *The Journal of Philosophy,* LIV, 8: 197–207, 1957.

— "Heidegger's 'Being,'" *The Journal of Philosophy,* XLIX: 415–422, 1952.

Hegel, G. W. F. *The Logic of Hegel.* London: Oxford University Press, 1931.

Heidegger, Martin. *Sein und Zeit.* Tübingen: 7. Aufl., 1953.

— *Vom Wesen des Grundes.* Halle: Niemeyer, 1929.

— *Kant und das Problem der Metaphysik.* Bonn: Cohen, 1929.

— *Was ist Metaphysik?* Bonn: Cohen, 1930.

— *Die Selbstbehauptung der deutschen Universität.* Breslau: Korn, 1933.

— *Hölderlin und das Wesen der Dichtung.* München: Langen, 1937.

– *Vom Wesen der Wahrheit*. Frankfurt a/M: Klostermann, 1943.
– *Erläuterungen zu Hölderlins Dichtung*. Frankfurt a/M: Klostermann, 1944.
– *Platons Lehre von der Wahrheit*. *Mit einem Brief über den "Humanismus."*
  Bern: Francke, 1947.
– *Holzwege*. Frankfurt a/M: Klostermann, 1950.
– *Der Feldweg*. Frankfurt a/M: Klostermann, 1953.
– *Einführung in die Metaphysik*. Tübingen: Niemeyer, 1953.
– *Was heisst Denken?* Tübingen: Niemeyer, 1954.
– *Aus der Erfahrung des Denkens*. Pfullingen: Neske, 1954.
– *Vorträge und Aufsätze*. Pfullingen: Neske, 1954.
– *Was ist das – die Philosophie?* Pfullingen: Neske, 1956.
– *Zur Seinsfrage*. Frankfurt a/M: Klostermann, 1956.
– *Der Satz vom Grund*. Pfullingen: Neske, 1957.
– *Identität und Differenz*. Pfullingen: Neske, 1957.
– *Hebel – Der Hausfreund*. Pfullingen: Neske, 1957.
– *Unterwegs zur Sprache*. Pfullingen: Neske, 1959.
– *Nietzsche*. 2 vols. Pfullingen: Neske, 1961.
– *Kants These über das Sein*. Frankfurt a/M: Klostermann, 1962.
– *Die Frage nach dem Ding*. Tübingen: Niemeyer, 1962.
– *Die Frage nach der Technik*. Pfullingen: Neske, 1962.
Hofstadter, Albert. *Truth and Art*. New York: Columbia University Press, 1965.
– "The Truth of Being," *The Journal of Philosophy*, LXII, 7:167–183, 1965.
Husserl, Edmund. *Ideas*. London: George Allen and Unwin Ltd., 1952.
– *Cartesian Meditations*. The Hague: Nijhoff, 1964.
– *The Idea of Phenomenology*. The Hague: Nijhoff, 1964.
– *Phenomenology and the Crisis of Philosophy*. New York: Harper & Row,
  1965.
Jaspers, Karl. *Nietzsche: Einführung in das Verständnis seines Philosophierens*.
  Berlin & Leipzig: De Gruyter, 1950.
Kant, Immanuel. *Critique of Pure Reason*. Trans. Norm Kemp Smith. New
  York and London: Macmillan, 1933.
– *Prolegomena to Any Future Metaphysics*. Trans. L. W. Beck. New York:
  Bobbs-Merrill, 1950.
– *Critique of Practical Reason*. Trans. L. W. Beck. New York: Bobbs-Merrill,
  1956.
– *Foundations of the Metaphysics of Morals*. Trans. L. W. Beck. New York:
  Bobbs-Merrill, 1959.
Kanthack, Katharina. *Das Denken Martin Heideggers*. Berlin: de Gruyter, 1959.
Kaufmann, Walter A. *Nietzsche: Philosopher, Psychologist, Antichrist*. Prince-
  ton University Press, 1950.
King, Magda. *Heidegger's Philosophy*. New York: Macmillan, 1964.
Kirk, G. S. and Raven, J. E. *The Presocratic Philosophers*. Cambridge: Cam-
  bridge University Press, 1960.
Langan, Thomas. *The Meaning of Heidegger*. New York: Columbia University
  Press, 1959.
Lauer, Quentin. *Phenomenology: Its Genesis and Prospect*. New York: Harper
  and Row, 1965.
Leibniz, Gottfried W. *Monadology and Other Philosophical Essays*. Trans. P.
  and A. Schrecker. New York: Bobbs-Merrill, 1965.
– *Discourse on Metaphysics*. Trans. Lucas and Grint. Manchester: University
  of Manchester Press, 1953.

Löwith, Karl. *Heidegger: Denker in Dürftiger Zeit.* Frankfurt a/M: Fischer, 1953.

– *Nietzsches Philosophie der ewigen Wiederkehr des Gleichen.* Stuttgart: Kohlhammer, 1956.

Macomber, W. B. *The Anatomy of Disillusion.* Evanston: Northwestern University Press, 1967.

Marx, Werner. *Heidegger und die Tradition.* Stuttgart: Kohlhammer, 1961.

Morgan, George A. *What Nietzsche Means.* Cambridge: Harvard University Press, 1941.

Nahm, Milton C. *Selections from Early Greek Philosophy.* New York: Appleton-Century-Crofts, 1934.

Nietzsche, Friedrich. *Grossoktavausgabe.* (1st ed.) 15 vols. Leipzig: C. G. Naumann, 1895–1901.

– *Grossoktavausgabe.* (2d ed.) 19 vols. Leipzig: 1901–1913.

– *Grossoktavausgabe.* (2d rev. ed.) 20 vols. Leipzig: R. Kröner, 1926.

– *Kleinoktavausgabe.* 16 vols. Leipzig: R. Kröner, 1899–1912.

– *Taschenausgabe.* 11 vols. Leipzig: C. G. Naumann and R. Kröner, 1906.

– *Werke in drei Bänden.* Karl Schlechta (ed.) München: Hanser, 1959–1961.

– *Nietzsche Index zu den Werken in drei Bänden.* Karl Schlechta. München: Hanser, 1965.

Oehler, Richard. *Friedrich Nietzsche und die Vorsokratiker.* Leipzig: Dürr, 1904.

Plato. *The Dialogues of Plato.* Trans. B. Jowett. 2 vols. New York: Random House, 1937.

– *The Republic of Plato.* Trans. F. M. Cornford. London: Oxford University Press, 1941.

– *Plato's Theory of Knowledge.* Trans. F. M. Cornford. New York: Bobbs-Merrill, 1957.

– *Plato and Parmenides.* Trans. F. M. Cornford. New York: Bobbs-Merrill, n.d.

– *Plato's Cosmology.* Trans. F. M. Cornford. New York: Bobbs-Merrill, n.d.

– *Plato's Phaedo.* Trans. R. Hackforth. Cambridge: Cambridge University Press, 1955.

– *Euthyphro, Apology, Crito.* Trans. R. D. Cummings. New York: Bobbs-Merrill, 1948.

– *Plato's Phaedrus.* Trans. R. Hackforth. Cambridge: Cambridge University Press, 1952.

Richardson, William. *Heidegger: Through Phenomenology to Thought.* The Hague: Nijhoff, 1963.

Schmitt, Richard. *Martin Heidegger on Being Human.* New York: Random House, 1969.

Schopenhauer, Arthur. *The World as Will and Idea.* 3 vols. Trans. R. B. Haldane and J. Kemp. London: 1906.

Seidel, Georg J. *Martin Heidegger and the Pre-Socratics.* Nebraska: University of Nebraska Press, 1964.

Simmel, Georg. *Schopenhauer und Nietzsche: Ein Vortragszyklus.* Leipzig: Dunker and Humblot, 1907.

Spiegelberg, Herbert. *The Phenomenological Movement.* 2 vols. The Hague: Nijhoff, 1960.

Spinoza, Baruch. *Ethics and On the Improvement of the Understanding.* New York: Hafner, 1955.

Vaihinger, Hans. *Die Philosophie Als-Ob.* Leipzig: Meiner, 1911.

Versenyi, Laszlo. *Heidegger, Being and Truth*. New Haven: Yale University Press, 1965.

Vietta, Egon. *Die Seinsfrage bei Martin Heidegger*. Stuttgart: C. E. Schwab, 1950.

Vycinas, Vincent. *Earth and Gods*. The Hague: Nijhoff, 1963.

Windelband, Wilhelm. *A History of Philosophy*. 2 vols. New York: Harper and Row, 1958.

Wiplinger, Fridolin. *Wahrheit und Geschichtlichkeit*. München: Alber, 1961.

INDEX